4th BN. WILTS. H.G.
O R.to.Ordnance

CEILING 3450   STRENGTH 305

COMPANY	No OF SECTION	No IN PLATOON	LOCATION	CEILING STRENGTH	ACTUAL STRENGTH	RIFLES	300 EY RIFLES	303 EY RIFLES	22 RIFLES	BAR	STEN	.305	LMG	BMG	VMG	S.MORTAR	SMITH GUN	2 PDR GUN	W/T	M/CYCLES	10 MEN PACKS
A	4	10	BN H Q	20	18											(8)	(3)	(2)	2	1	127
A	-	1	TROWBRIDGE	635	626	247	8	7	(4)	-	109		8	-		(8)	(3)	(2)	2	1	
	1		WESTWOOD	100	105		2						2	-							
	2		LIMPLEY STOKE	40	32								1								
	3		WINSLEY	60	55		2						1			(3)					
B	4		MONKTON FARLEIGH	30	40		4														
	5		SOUTH WRAXALL	30	48								1								
	6		HOLT	80	92			7	1	107		6		2		(2)					70
	7		STAVERTON	50	52		8	(70)	2	145		8	1			(3)	(3)	(3)		1	(13)
C	9	23	COY TOTAL / MELKSHAM	590 / 650	+23 / 550	200 / 240	8 / 21														(7)
D	5	+	DEVIZES	+82	322	132	2	3	(7)	-	122	2	5	1	1	(2)	(2)	(2)	5	1	(7)
E	1		UPTON, MARKET LAVINGTON	87	77						15		2			(2)	(1)				
	2		TILSHEAD, WEST LAVINGTON	103	59						22		1			(2)	(1)				
	3		THE CHEVERELLS	50	57					7	15		1			(2)	(3)				
	4	12	COY TOTAL	240	210	109	8	-	7	2	50	4	4		1	(2)	(3)		1	1	42
F	1		BROMHAM	20	90								2			(3)	(3)	(2)			
	2		SEEND	65	79						7		2	2		(3)	(5)				
	3		STEEPLE ASHTON	103	104						7	2	1	1		(3)	(5)				
	4		WORTON	75	72						7		1			(2)	(3)				
	5		POTTERNE	100	92						21		4			(5)	(2)	(2)			
G	20		COY TOTAL	433	441	264	9	3	9+	3	44	2	7	1	1	(5)(4)	(0)	(2)	-	-	95
G	1		BISHOPS CANNINGS	75	78						7		2			(0)					
	2		MARDEN	65	73			5	1	7		1		2		(0)	(2)				
	3		URCHFONT	40	41			5	1	7		1				(0)					
	4	9	COY TOTAL	180	184	121	10	2	5	1	21	4	4	2	-	(5)(4)	(2)			1	47
H	4	12	BRADFORD ON AVON	420	271	81	19	10	85		85	-	45	1	5	(5)	(9)		2	-	64
*	42	82	BN TOTAL	3450	3023	1527	81	34	90	2	792	2	47	7	5	(3)(9)			4	9	638

Location, strength and arms of The 4th Battalion Wiltshire Home Guard.

THE HISTORY OF
THE WILTSHIRE HOME GUARD

Edited by

MAJOR E. A. MACKAY, T.D., D.L., J.P.

(Secretary of The Wiltshire County Territorial Association,
1939-45)

The Naval & Military Press Ltd

Published by

The Naval & Military Press Ltd
Unit 10 Ridgewood Industrial Park,
Uckfield, East Sussex,
TN22 5QE England

Tel: +44 (0) 1825 749494
Fax: +44 (0) 1825 765701

www.naval-military-press.com
www.nmarchive.com

FOREWORD

(From General The Hon. Sir Francis Gathorne-Hardy, Lockeridge House, Marlborough, Wilts.)

THE Home Guard, or the Local Defence Volunteers as they were originally called, came into being when these islands were faced with a disaster which had already overwhelmed much of Europe, and when we were left alone to oppose the victorious enemy. At the hour in May 1940 when the call for a citizen defence force went out, there were some who felt that the response might not be as wholehearted as the situation demanded. These pessimists were rapidly confounded. The appeal from the very first day met with an enthusiastic response throughout the length and breadth of the country.

Nowhere was the response more enthusiastic than in the county of Wiltshire.

Recruits poured in from both town and country, and the Home Guard soon proved itself to be the greatest and the most successful volunteer movement in our long history.

In the early days the demands on the time and energy of the recruits were very heavy. The necessities of drill, musketry, field operations and even night duties were onerous and mostly fell on men who were already working full time, and often more, in their peace-time occupations.

The demands were met with the maximum of enthusiasm and the minimum of grumbling. In consequence the efficiency of the volunteer force soon reached a high level.

The age limit forced me to resign from the Home Guard before it was disbanded but I know and shall always be proud to remember, that I handed over to my successor a highly efficient body of men who bore a vital part in the defence schemes of the British Isles.

F. G. H.

Lockeridge, 23 Jan. 1946.

FOREWORD

by

Colonel His Grace The Duke of Somerset, D.S.O., O.B.E.

Lord Lieutenant of Wiltshire and Home Guard Adviser

To all those interested in Wiltshire I would like to commend to their notice this book, entitled *The History of the Wiltshire Home Guard*, compiled by Major E. A. Mackay.

Major Mackay, as Secretary of the Territorial Association in Wiltshire, has had more to do with the formation, equipping and organisation of the Home Guard than any one else in the county, for all the work done in connection with the Home Guard has been done from Territorial Army Headquarters.

Major Mackay is very patriotically giving the profits from the sale of this book to the funds of the Wiltshire Regiment O.C.A., and I hope those who read it will appreciate the work that Major Mackay has done in connection with the Home Guard, and I am sure they will be very interested in its contents.

SOMERSET

3 *Dec.* 1945.

THE BROADCAST APPEAL WHICH CALLED THE
L.D.V INTO BEING
Delivered by Mr. Anthony Eden on 14 May, 1940

" I WANT to speak to you to-night," said Mr. Eden, " about the form of warfare which the Germans have been employing so successfully against Holland and Belgium—namely, the dropping of troops by parachute behind the main defence lines." He then explained that the purpose of the parachutist is to disorganise and confuse, as a preparation for the landing of troops by aircraft.

" In order to leave nothing to chance," Mr. Eden went on, " and to supplement resources as yet untapped and the means of defence already arranged, we are going to ask you to help us in a manner which I hope will be welcome to thousands of you. Since the war began, the Government has received countless inquiries from all over the Kingdom, from men of all ages who are, for one reason or another, not at present engaged in military service and who wish to do something for the defence of the country.

" Now is your opportunity. We want large numbers of such men in Great Britain who are British subjects, between the ages of 15 and 65, to come forward now and offer their services in order to make assurance doubly sure. The name of the new Force which is now to be raised will be the Local Defence Volunteers. This name describes its duties in three words. You will not be paid, but you will receive uniform and you will be armed. In order to volunteer what you have to do is to give in your names at your local Police Station, and then, as and when we want you, we will let you know."

THE KING'S BROADCAST TO THE HOME GUARD

Reprinted from " The Times," Monday 4 Dec. 1944

Last night the King broadcast to the Home Guard a message in which he expressed his own and the nation's thanks for their " steadfast devotion," which had " helped much to ward off the danger of invasion."

His Majesty said :

Over four years ago, in May, 1940, our country was in mortal danger. The most powerful army the world had ever seen had forced its way to within a few miles of our coast. From day to day we were threatened with invasion.

In those days our Army had been gravely weakened. A call went out for men to enrol themselves in a new citizen army, the Local Defence Volunteers, ready to use whatever weapons could be found and to stand against the invader in every village and every town. Throughout Britain and Northern Ireland the nation answered that summons, as free men will always answer when freedom is in danger. From fields and hills, from factories and mills, from shops and offices, men of every age and every calling came forward to train themselves for battle. Almost over-night, a new force came into being, a force which had little equipment but was mighty in courage and determination.

In July, 1940, the Local Defence Volunteers became the Home Guard. During those four years of continuing anxiety that civilian army grew in strength ; under the competent administration of the Territorial Army Associations, it soon became a well-equipped and capable force, able to take over many duties from regular soldiers preparing to go overseas. I believe it is the voluntary spirit which has always made the Home Guard so splendid and so powerful a comradeship of arms. The hope that this comradeship will long endure was strong in me this afternoon while many thousands of you marched past me in one of the most impressive and memorable parades that I have ever seen.

For most of you—and, I must add, for your wives too your service in the Home Guard has not been easy. I know what it has meant, especially for older men. Some of you have stood for many hours on the gun sites, in desolate fields, or wind-swept beaches. Many of you, after a long and hard day's work, scarcely had time for food before you changed into uniform for the evening parade. Some of you had to bicycle for long distances to the drill hall or the rifle range.

It was well known to the enemy that if he came to any part of our land he would meet determined opposition, at every point in his advance, from men who had good weapons, and, better still, knew how to use them. In that way the existence of the Home Guard helped much to ward off the danger of invasion. Then, too, our own plans for campaigns in many parts of the world depended on our having a great citizen force to help in the defence of the homeland. As anti-

8

aircraft and coastal gunners, sentries at vulnerable points, units for dealing with unexploded bombs, and in many other ways, the Home Guard have played a full part in the defence of their country. Many will remember with special gratitude the unsparing help given to the Civil Defence Services in days and nights of terror and destruction.

But you have gained something for yourselves. You have discovered in yourselves new capabilities. You have found how men from all kinds of homes and many different occupations can work together in a great cause, and how happy they can be with each other. That is a memory and a knowledge which may help us all in the many peace-time problems that we shall have to tackle before long.

I am very proud of what the Home Guard has done and I give my heartfelt thanks to you all. Officers, non-commissioned officers, and men, you have served your country with a steadfast devotion. I know that your country will not forget that service.

" ESSENTIAL PART IN DEFENCE "

His Majesty's Message in Army Orders

A Special Army Order was issued to the Home Guard, with the following message rom the King, on 3 Dec. 1944 :

For more than four years you have borne a heavy burden. Most of you have been engaged for long hours in work necessary to the prosecution of the war or to maintaining the healthful life of the nation ; and you have given a great portion of the time which should have been your own to learning the skilled work of a soldier. By this patient, ungrudging effort you have built and maintained a force able to play an essential part in the defence of our threatened soil and liberty.

I have long wished to see you relieved of this burden ; but it would have been a betrayal of all we owe to our fathers and our sons if any step had been taken which might have imperilled our country's safety. Till very recently, a slackening of our defences might have encouraged the enemy to launch a desperate blow which could grievously have damaged us and weakened the power of our own assault. Now, at last, the splendid resolution and endurance of the allied armies have thrust back that danger from our coasts. At last I can say that you have fulfilled your charge.

The Home Guard has reached the end of its long tour of duty under arms. But I know that your devotion to our land, your comradeship, your power to work your hardest at the end of the longest day will discover new outlets for patriotic service in time of peace.

History will say that your share in the greatest of all our struggles for freedom was a vitally important one. You have given your service without thought of reward. You have earned in full measure your country's gratitude.

GEORGE R.I., Colonel-in-Chief.

9

THE HOME GUARD OF ENGLAND

THE Trained Bands of Elizabeth ; the Somerset men raised against Monmouth ; the Fencibles of the north ; the Militia and Yeomanry and the Loyal Corps of Infantry of the south, raised to repel the invasion of Bonaparte ; the National Reserve of the last Great War, and now the Home Guard.

Truly a wonderful cavalcade. Stout hearts determined to defend their beloved England to their last breath. Stay-at-home brothers of the men of Raleigh, Marlborough, Wellington and Haig — patriots to the backbone, grousing a little, swearing a little, denying themselves much, worthy components of the stained-glass glory of the chivalry of England.

After the Great World War, those of us who studied the trend of world affairs, even in the most dilettante fashion, felt our own impotence in the face of a policy which not only omitted to face up to the inevitable, but cut down our services, and even skimped our devoted Territorials of the cost of training—Then came Munich ; " Peace in our time." Had we been mistaken ?

The storm clouds thickened and broke ; six months of " the phoney war " in France ; Britain not yet even roused—then the avalanche, rumours of dreadful happenings, we were almost numbed. Came the evening of May 14, 1940, a call to arms of every man between the ages of 17 and 65 : an electrifying broadcast from the Secretary of State for War, Mr. Anthony Eden—a broadcast that not only altered the lives and outlook of millions of men in this country, but which possibly altered the course of history.

The Local Defence Volunteers were born. Voluntary, unpaid, equipped (and how equipped !) for the duration of the war. A cynic has written that the L.D.V. was the illegitimate child of the Police foisted on the Army !

The fact remains that the Police were very much in the picture at the start. Not only did they contact the most suitable retired officers in their districts to organise the force, but they drew and distributed rifles—a very few—and armbands—our only equipment at first, they borrowed shot-guns from trusting owners and they took and vetted the names of the multitudes who flocked to the Police Stations.

Then meetings were advertised. From hamlet, village, town, villa and factory poured the volunteers. They gathered in squares, market-places and fields ; they elected leaders and instructors ; they divided up into squads, platoons and companies, and every evening they were marched, drilled and instructed by those with former experience, the old soldiers " back to the Army again," the very backbone of our country. Soon uniforms began to arrive, meetings were held of the leading ex-officers of the counties, battalion and company commanders appointed ; the first schemes worked out for the defence of roads and towns, hasty defences contrived, carts in readiness to block roads, armed sentries to question passers by, and guards mounted at road blocks and vulnerable points.

Those were exciting and exacting days.

During their vigils they watched the Battle of Britain rage—they saw history made. Towns and countryside were ablaze with searchlights and many an enemy bomber did the watchers glimpse in the beams. Happy nights, too, in a way, for in them was forged the great comradeship between the men—class was forgotten in this great English brotherhood, all were hoping that they were not too late to gain the knowledge that would help them to do their part when the Hunnish hordes, now reformed after Dunkirk, crossed the narrow seas and hurled their hellish might on our beloved land.

And now into the picture on June 24, 1940, came the Territorial Army Associations.

Deserted by their elder wards, the Territorial Battalions, reduced to skeleton staffs, small in numbers but efficient and experienced, on them was placed the sudden burden of organising and administering the million and a half men in many thousands of places from end to end of the country, now designated the Home Guard. The Territorial Directorate of the War Office became also the Home Guard Directorate, military channels of training and supply were sorted out and soon the Associations were wrestling with the problems of clothing, equipment, arms, ammunition, training manuals and accommodation for this vast mushroom army—arms poured in from the United States.

Mistakes were, of course, made, but gradually order was achieved by super-human effort, and the parts of the great machine fitted together.

By September 15, when invasion seemed imminent, the force had begun to find itself, and after that, training went on apace and always the old soldiers showed their worth—but there was very little jealousy and they were only too keen to train younger men to bear their part of the burden.

The work of all ranks was a veritable saga of self-denial, at first totally unpaid they came often from farm and factory direct to their posts and back again in the morning.

Gradually further and wonderful weapons were issued ; the historic pike, Molotoff cocktails, bomb projectors, gradually superseded by weapons and explosives of greater power and use, machine-guns, spigot mortars, two-pounder anti-tank guns, six-pounders, anti-tank mines, to mention a few.

Men were drafted from general service battalions to man " Z " Batteries, rocket projectors, which shot down their quota of enemy planes.

Light anti-aircraft guns were manned to guard factories and vulnerable points.

Full time officers were provided as battalion adjutants, quartermasters and training officers ; ranges equipped, better accommodation provided, magazines built and permanent staff instructors supplied, and all the time the wave of paper mounted—the very *bete noire* of the life of the harassed officers—so that paid company clerks had to be employed to deal with the mass of transfers, etc.

An Order in Council was issued making service compulsory for men not otherwise employed in the various services. This was taken in good part, and the men so directed by the labour exchanges were trained by the devoted training cadres of their companies.

The financial side of the force settled into shape, a Capitation Grant paying for salaries, office expences and various purchases. The other items, such as subsistence, travelling allowance, minor works and training grant, being met from other votes. This was all administered by the Territorial Associations.

And so this younger brother of our national forces grew up. Varied much by circumstance and locality but united by its solid determination to hold the fort, not unworthily, when our army of invasion left these shores, and ready, if need be to resist with all its might any invader who dared to sully our fair country with his foul foot, looking back a little wistfully to the time when, ill-armed and part equipped, it bade defiance to the enemy in our hour of greatest peril.

Its happiest memory in future will be the wonderful bonds of comradeship between all ranks, its proudest moment when it heard the words of our great Prime Minister, " Home Guards, guard well our homes."

THE HOME GUARD OF WILTSHIRE

AND so it was in our County of Wiltshire. Directly the chance of helping England was heard on the wireless the police stations throughout the county were besieged by telephone calls and by callers. The village inns did a roaring trade that night, and next morning the bewildered Police, some of whom had not heard the news, were hard put to it—sorting out applications and politely sifting out those who did not appear to conform to the very wide conditions of service.

Throughout the whole time the Police of the county did magnificent work, collecting and distributing arms and ammunition of every sort, not only those issued by authority but the shotguns and variety of weapons lent by private owners.

And still the men came in. In three days, excluding Salisbury, the number mounted to 3,754 ;

From north to south ; from east to west they came.

From Cricklade to Tollard Royal ; from Ditteridge to Buttermere ; from Clyffe Pypard, Lydiard Tregoze, Teffont Magna, Clarendon and Zeals.

Names recalling the great days of Old England. Villages whose men had gone to Agincourt, Crecy, Waterloo, Neuve Chapelle, who had served under Drake, Raleigh, Marlborough, Roberts and Haig.

Men of great names, too, Bolingbroke, Essex, Leicester, Stanley, Pembroke and Somerset.

Names woven into the tapestry that is England.

Our beginnings were very humble. Headquarters of companies, platoons, and even of battalions were located in houses and rooms begged or borrowed, in stables, outhouses and bar-parlours. Only later did our most helpful quartering commandants appear on the scene. Lt.-Col. C. Smyth Piggott for the north and Lt.-Col. F. N. Jeans for the south of the county. By their good offices accommodation was requisitioned and rooms were hired for offices, stores and training.

The Territorial Drill Halls had been taken for the Army, but in course of time they were returned for the use of the Home Guard, the new name for the force, substituted in July 1940 for the honoured name of the Local Defence Volunteers.

Makeshift also were our look-out posts. Shepherds' vans were much in demand and others were made locally with boards and rabbit netting.

Our primitive road-blocks were things to look back at with a shudder.

One dreads to think what would have been their fate if they had really been put to the test.

Farm carts and wired knife-rests, covered by fire from trenches were all that we had.

But we did what we could in the haste that was with us night and day, for, in a short month or so, Holland had been invaded, France had fallen, and our Army, left in the lurch, came back to us from Dunkirk.

13

It was up to us to hold the fort while they reorganised. Our pitiful supply of arms had been augmented by ·300 rifles, Lewis Guns and Thompson sub-machine-guns—" Tommy " guns—from America. The rifles had last seen the light of day when they had been packed away after the last war in grease of an incredible hardness which took all our energy to clean.

And we had our Molotov cocktails, creosote and paraffin in bottles, home made incendiary bombs.

These had done good work when used by the Finns against the Russians.

Our village greens, football fields and meadows every night resounded to the words of command of instructors—fine men from the last war, the salt of England —who were teaching the rudiments of drill, musketry and bombing. Elementary tactical classes were held and the countryside erupted bunches of elderly men training in field work.

On June 4, Mr. Winston Churchill, our great Prime Minister, delivered the most impressive broadcast of all time. " We shall not flag nor fail ; we shall go on to the end ; we shall fight . . . we shall defend our island whatever the cost may be. We shall fight on the beaches, the landing grounds, in the fields, in the streets and on the hills. We shall never surrender."

He was saying what was in our hearts.

And later, " Behind the Regular Army we have more than a million of the L.D.V. or, as they are much better called, the Home Guard. We shall defend every village, every town, every city."

So now we were the Home Guard.

The Battle of Britain was on. Night after night, watching from our posts, we saw the searchlights combing the sky. We heard the threatening intermittent throb of the enemy planes, the cheering roar of our night fighters in pursuit.

On September 15 came the culmination, the day on which England was saved, when our Spitfires shot down 184 enemy planes from the sky—that night was one of tension. Enemy forces were reported as massed in landing craft in the ports of France.

Then came the Navy's turn, the narrow seas were kept inviolate.

We had been half dreading to hear the church bells ring, the signal that the enemy were in our midst.

By the grace of God, and our gallant lads, they were never rung, till, many months later, one Sunday morning, during an exercise, we heard them ringing for morning service, and a good sound it was. The danger of invasion was averted.

Time went on, the Home Guard was growing up, clothing, equipment, arms and explosives of all sorts poured in ; Northovers, spigot mortars, machine-guns, Sten guns, bombs of various sorts had to be learned and taught. Risky work, some of it, but on the whole we were very lucky and accidents were few.

Before long administrative assistants were appointed to help us with the ever increasing paper work, these were later supplanted by adjutants and quarter-masters, to each battalion, and in time training officers came to us, all keen to help us with our training programmes and exercises. They had to work hard, too, as all our work had to be done in the evenings and at the week-ends.

Somehow, most of our difficulties were overcome and we emerged passably trained and by this time fully confident that we could give a good account of ourselves if the occasion arose.

We became more ambitious, twenty-four hour exercises were staged, battles fought against neighbouring companies, then regular troops, and, as time went on against our allies from the U.S.A. who were only too willing to " play " with us and to help us in every way. We feel that we have made some real friends among them.

The original scheme of O.P.s and strong points at road junctions had given way to a concerted system of " defence in depth " all over the county and all over the country, town defences were set up, consisting of road blocks, strengthened by steel rails set into the ground, and country platoons formed into flying columns ; some regular columns were standing by to reinforce.

The name " tank island " was used for towns defended in this way.

A feature of this period was the close co-operation between the Home Guard and the Civil Defence Services, who by now were fully organised to meet every eventuality except actual fighting. Many of the wardens were old soldiers who had obeyed the first call to the help of their country, to serve as air-raid wardens, and one may be sure that they would have snatched up a rifle and fought alongside us if the occasion had arisen.

The years passed, and so did the chance of invasion ; Hitler was hard pressed and had lost his chance.

Early in 1944 our dispositions were altered again, road blocks were demolished and our duties were to be ready to sally forth and engage any enemy who might come by parachute, the duty for which we were originally formed.

It was a pleasant change to the road blocks and we took a great deal of interest in our field schemes again.

June 6, 1944 was the day on which our expeditionary force landed in Normandy and once again the thrill of our earlier days was with us, for our duty was to guard the railway bridges over which passed the trains carrying our troops and their vast supplies. Sabotage was always possible, but luckily there was no sign of it and, after a short time the guards were taken off.

As our armies pressed on and freed the countries so long in bondage to the Hun we began to realise more and more that our usefulness had passed and that England was free from the fear of invasion.

It was felt that the long strain had left many of us tired and so, in August, a month's holiday, except for musketry, was given.

Training was resumed but we all felt that the Home Guard was passing, we were warned of the code word which would herald our dissolution and, at the end of October, we knew that the " stand down " was fixed for November 1.

Heavy weapons, their ammunition, bombs, blankets etc., had already for the most part been withdrawn and the force was told that personal uniform, greatcoats and boots might be retained to become their own property, but that they had to be kept in a serviceable condition until the final disbandment.

A final parade was ordered for Sunday December 3 after which personal weapons, ammunition and all other equipment would be handed in, the final date being December 31.

Men were to be liable to recall if the " exigencies of the service "—that dread phrase—demanded it.

ORGANISATION

THE organisation of the ever-increasing numbers of Local Defence Volunteers was soon under way.

The Regional Commissioner got in touch with the Lord Lieutenant, Sir Ernest Wills, and the Chief Constable, Col. Hoël Llewellyn, later knighted, and the two latter approached Gen. The Hon. Sir J. Francis Gathorne Hardy, G.C.B., G.C.V.O., C.M.G., D.S.O., of Lockeridge House, Marlborough, a distinguished retired officer, and asked him to accept the post of Area Organiser, later known as Zone Organiser.

These three latter then held a meeting and divided the county by Police divisions, each division providing a group which later became a battalion, commanded by a group organiser.

All volunteers were at this time technically of equal status, military rank and commissions not being introduced until the Gazette of February 1, 1941.

On May 16, Gen. Gathorne Hardy invited the following retired officers to meet at Lockeridge House in order to fix up the command of the various groups, later battalions.

Col. The Hon. C. M. Hore-Ruthven, C.M.G., D.S.O.
Col. The Hon. A. F. Stanley, D.S.O.
Col. Sir George S. Herbert, Bt., G.C.V.O.
Brig.-Gen. The Lord Roundway, C.M.G., D.S.O., M.V.O.
Col. B. L. Birley, D.S.O.
Maj.-Gen. W. P. H. Hill, C.M.G., D.S.O.
Maj.-Gen. G.H.B. Freeth, C.B., C.M.G., D.S.O.
Brig.-Gen. H. F. E. Lewin, C.B., C.M.G.
Lt.-Col. W. C. H. Bell, D.S.O.
Admiral Hyde Parker

The meeting was also attended by

Maj. E. A. Mackay, T.D., Secretary of the Wiltshire
County Territorial Army Association
Mr. A. R. Alderton, Assistant Secretary

The Territorial Army Association was not as yet officially responsible for the supplies and administration of the Local Defence Volunteers but this followed in July.

The group—later battalion—commands were now as follows :

No. 1. Chippenham, Col. Hore-Ruthven, who handed over to Brig.-Gen. C. R. B. Carrington on being recalled for service, and later came back as Second in Command ; **No. 2. Malmesbury,** Col. Stanley ; **No. 3. Warminster,** Col. Sir George Herbert ; **No. 4. Trowbridge and Devizes,** Brig.-Gen. Lord Roundway ; **No. 5. Swindon,** Col. Birley ; **No. 6. Marlborough,** Gen. Gathorne Hardy, who on his higher appointment handed over to Capt. A. L. F. Fuller ; **No. 7. Bulford,** Maj.-Gen. Hill, who, owing to ill-health, shortly handed over to Major A. E. Phillips, D.S.O.

On October 1 the Sarum City Company of the 7th Battalion was formed into **No. 8. Salisbury,** Maj.-Gen. G. H. B. Freeth, C.B., C.M.B., D.S.O. and very shortly No. 5 Battalion was centred in Swindon Borough and **No. 9. Swindon Division,** Brig.-Gen. Lewin was recruited from the surrounding country, and **No. 10. Pewsey,** Col. Bell, was formed from the Marlborough Battalion.

The above were the original Local Defence Volunteer battalions, but during the course of the war further battalions were formed as follows :

No. 11. S. Marston, on the arrival of Messrs. Shortt Bros., Lt.-Col. M. O. Darby, O.B.E. ; **No. 12. Corsham,** composed of employees of the Bristol Aeroplane Co. formed in 1943, Lt.-Col. C. H. Tucker, and **No. 13. Swindon,** formed by the G.W.R. in the same year, Lt.-Col. S. A. Dyer.

In addition to these there was an M.T. Company at Salisbury commanded by Maj. F. R. Way, O.B.E., and a rocket (Z) battery near Swindon, the personnel being drafted from the 5th, 9th and 11th Battalions, trained and directed by a regular staff of the Anti-aircraft Command.

On February 1, 1941, commissions were granted to Home Guard officers, and Gen. Gathorne Hardy was appointed Zone Commander.

In these duties he was assisted by Maj. J. H. Clay until his retirement in 1942, an event regretted by everyone.

In the same gazette the first ten above-mentioned battalion commanders were confirmed in their appointments.

The county was divided into North and South Groups on May 1, 1941, Lord Roundway being given the North Group and being succeeded in the command of the 4th Battalion by Brig. Darwell. Gen. Freeth commanded the South Group and handed over the 8th Battalion to Gen. Sir H. Martelli.

In March 1942 Lord Roundway was appointed Zone Commander, with Maj. W. H. E. Thomas as his assistant. This designation was altered to Group Commander, North and South Groups being abolished. He held this position until his much lamented death on March 29, 1944, when the appointment was abolished.

The appointment of Home Guard Adviser was then introduced, as Home Guard liaison officer with Salisbury Plain District.

This duty was undertaken by Col. His Grace The Duke of Somerset, D.S.O., O.B.E.

In April 1942 compulsion was introduced, this, of course, necessitated the formation of several of the battalions already mentioned.

While on this subject it is interesting to note that battalions were still recruited from Police divisions, irrespective of numbers. Therefore it was quite on the cards that a single company in one strong battalion might outnumber another complete battalion. At Stand Down one company numbered 635 officers and men !

In July 1943 the county was divided into sectors, these were for operational purposes only and worked under Salisbury Plain District. They were commanded by Home Guard officers and had their own staffs, including a serving adjutant.

They were as follows :

N.E. Sector, Col. F. W. Wilson FitzGerald, D.S.O., M.C.

S. Sector, Brig. H. St. G. Schomberg, D.S.O.

W. Sector, Col. A. H. Burn, C.I.E., O.B.E.

Actually Col. Burn was a serving officer, commanding troops at Corsham.

All the above officers, with the exception of Col. Burn, had Home Guard commissions.

Operationally the forces was under the command of Salisbury Plain Area, later named District, who also controlled the distribution of arms and ammunition, the actual work of which was done by the Territorial Army Association under their direction.

Their sympathy, advice and help was always ours for the asking and, if various regulations, orders and counter-orders did cause us to query the wisdom of some of our superiors, we were pretty sure that it was none of District's doing.

As time went on we were given help from the Forces in our training and ever-increasing paper work.

At an early date an administrative assistant was allowed for each battalion. These were in some cases Home Guard Officers, and so well did they carry out their duties, some were taken on by the Army and later developed into A. & Q. officers.

These administrative assistants were paid by special grant to Territorial Army Associations.

In November 1940 permanent staff instructors were appointed, these finally totalled about four per large battalion, and well they worked.

January 1942 brought us adjutants and quartermasters, just in time to save the reason of harrassed C.O.s and a hard and difficult job they had, no blowing " orderly sergeants " and getting the job put in hand at once, but infinite patience in tactfully persuading part-time officers, often with no previous military experience, to render reports about men or material which, possibly by reason of harvest work or sickness, they could only trace with an expenditure of time that they simply did not possess. And they very likely filled up the form wrongly after all !

Training officers arrived in due course, one to every two or three battalions, of the greatest help in arranging schemes and exercises, and some very good shows they stage-managed.

Troops stationed in the county, both British and American, were always ready to " co-operate " and to lend us instructors and vehicles. They really took an interest in our strange force and we made many friends among them.

THE T.A.

In 1907, when Mr. Haldane, as Secretary of State for War, converted the old Volunteers into the Territorial Army, County Associations were appointed to administer and to help in their accommodation, recruiting and general well-being.

These were directly responsible to the War Office and were composed of Military Members representing Territorial units in the county, representative members, appointed by the County Council and four co-opted members. They were mostly ex-officers.

The Lord Lieutenant was ex-officio President.

In 1939, on the embodiment of the County Units, the Territorial Army Association of Wiltshire was left with only the care of the various Territorial drill halls in the county. The staff was reduced to a skeleton one, consisting only of the Secretary, Assistant Secretary, and one lady clerk.

When the Local Defence Volunteers was raised they at once offered their services, but it was not till a month or so had gone by that they were appointed the official guardians of the new force which much complicated their work in sorting out the various issues that had already been made.

The whole thing was such a new experience for everyone that we had to feel our way and improvise as best we could when the occasion arose, and everything had to be done in a hurry. Taking all in all it is surprising that the muddles were not even greater than they were.

As the work increased men with a knowledge of quartermaster duties, clerks and storemen, had to be found. The Association were fortunate in obtaining the services of experienced ex-W.O.s of the County Regiment.

Work was very heavy, hours very long, the job was complicated, but it was done with an enthusiasm that could not be defeated.

Caps, boots, denims and rifles in bulk began to come in during July. Ledgers were improvised and issues made with as much method as was possible.

Mr. Alderton, the Assistant Secretary, thought out the simplest methods for dealing with the mass of correspondence and forms which, sure enough, soon began to come along, although those at the top promised that they would be cut to a minimum. He later took on the especial task of finance, which was soon on us and increased daily like a snowball.

It was not always possible for him to see eye to eye with everyone in the matter of their claims, but his fairness and efficiency were the subject of many congratulatory remarks, and some idea of his work may be judged by the fact that the expenditure on the Home Guard up to March 1944 was about a quarter of a million pounds, and every penny accounted for.

Mr. Saxty joined us in January 1941 and in July took over the Q. side of the work as it had so grown that it could not be worked from one office. His was the complicated work of issuing and accounting for arms, clothing, equipment, ammunition, stores of all sorts, and for arranging their transport.

An arduous and complicated task, done with energy and thoroughness.

In July 1942 Maj. Lyne was released from active service and came back to the Association, taking on the issuing of clothing, equipment, medical and signalling stores.

Mr. Slatford joined us in 1941, taking charge of records, no mean task when one realises that numbers rose to nearly 25,000 when compulsory service had been introduced, transfers were continual, 15,271 had been discharged, and that by the end he was responsible for 39,427 enrolment forms.

Accommodation for training, offices, stores and ammunition had to be arranged and kept up ; this work was done with care and accuracy by Mr. Gayton.

By August 1941 the staff had increased to 16, and later to 26. Not excessive, considering that the numbers administered amounted to practically two divisions.

Mention must be made of the help that was given by Salisbury Plain Area later District, and especially by Capt. T. D. F. Macneal, the Staff Captain, whose wise advice was always freely given, and taken, and who has given us the following notes.

NOTES ON THE RELATION OF THE STAFF TO THE HOME GUARD

In June 1940, a separate Home Guard staff branch was created at Area H.Q.s. This branch consisted of a G.1 (Home Guard) (colonel), G.3 (captain) and staff captain (captain). These appointments were filled in most cases by officers with Territorial Army experience. This Home Guard staff branch dealt with all Home Guard matters ; keeping the Area Commander fully advised and so enabling him to fit the Home Guard into his plans for defence. On the " Q " side a close liaison was kept with the Territorial Army Association.

" G " matters included subjects such as tank islands and defended localities, signal communications, exercises, supervision of training, courses, ranges, training ammunition, etc.

" A " and " Q " covered commissions, promotions, resignations, disciplinary questions, courts of enquiry, provision of adjutants, captains, A Q.s and P.S.I.s. War Department vehicles and earmarked civilian transport, transport for personnel, feeding arrangements and ten man packs, operational ammunition, storehouses for explosives, etc.

During the first two years it was undoubtedly helpful to Home Guard commanders, while the Home Guard was forming, organising and being equipped, in being able to refer any matter to one staff branch.

By the middle of 1942, the Home Guard had become a formidable force. Training had gone on steadily, and the flow of arms and ammunition was increasing. The Army's link with the Home Guard was therefore reviewed.

Taking into account the important position the Home Guard now filled in home defence and the fact that this importance would grow as the Army went overseas, the Gale Commission recommended that the connection between the Home Guard and Army should be drawn closer. This it was thought would be assisted by abolishing the separate Home Guard staff branch and dealing with all Home Guard matters at area H.Q.s through the usual staff branches in exactly the same way as for the Army. This recommendation was adopted, though a G.1 (Home Guard) was retained as a liaison officer to advise the Commander on Home Guard questions, but without any executive power. This system remained in force until the Stand Down on 31st December, 1944.

(Signed) T. D. F. MACNEAL,
Capt.
Salisbury Plain District.

NOTES ON THE ISSUE OF WEAPONS

Personal Weapons

Shotguns must be placed first on the list, for these formed the majority of the weapons of the original Local Defence Volunteers. By July 1940 various owners had kindly lent 1,052 of these, by 1942 the number had increased to 1,746.

Bayonet Standards, the official name of the famous pikes, were issued to the number of 1,100, but probably very few of these were ever served out to the men.

Rifles, ·303. Delivery began in June 1940 and by the end of July we had 4,365, but these were shortly withdrawn and superseded by

Rifles, ·300 which were old American weapons from the last war, of three makes. 7,180 of these had arrived by September 1940 ; this number increased to 10,744 by December 1941.

Rifles, E.Y. 790 of these weapons were adapted for discharger cups for throwing grenades.

Rifles, ·22, also from America, totalled 400 by the end of 1942.

Thompson Sub-machine-guns, from America, came during 1941, totalling 506 in March, 1942, when they were taken for the Regular Army and

Sten Carbines, mass-poduced, handy automatic weapons, were issued in their place to the number of 2,993.

Lewis machine-guns totalled 280 by the end of 1941, other machine-guns included Brownings, Vickers and Marlins.

Revolvers, mostly privately owned, totalled 367.

Sub-Artillery

Northover Projector, very home-made in appearance but accurate and capable of throwing its own phosphorus bottles and hand grenades, was first on the scene in April 1941. By December 250 had been issued, but it then declined in favour and was replaced by

Spigot Mortars, a new type of anti-tank weapon which threw a heavy high explosive bomb accurately up to 200 yards. By October 1942, 328 of these were in our hands.

Smith Guns. 110 of these had been issued by the end of 1942, but were always regarded with a good deal of awe.

Flame Throwers to the number of 55 were held for the defence of road blocks— We always wondered what would happen if one were used.

Artillery

60-Pounder Guns. Two of these were issued and intended for the defence of Chippenham.

6-Pounders were coming in at a late date, but training never went very far.

6-inch Mortars. 4 of these were received towards the end.

By the end of 1942 every man either had a personal weapon or some specialist rôle. Every man was expected to be efficient in his own weapon and also in one other.

It is interesting to note that, when winding up the Home Guard, the Territoral Association dealt with 200 tons of light weapons and 250 tons of heavy weapons, these figures include all spares and accessories.

Strength of Personnel

In June 1940, 15,879 men had joined ; by December the strength was 17,194. These numbers remained very constant till the Autumn of 1942, when the conscripts started to come in. By the end of that year we had 20,650 men and by September 1943 our highest number was reached, namely 23,409. After this there was a slight decline, owing to men going to the services, our strength at Stand Down in December 1944 being 21,993.

Ammunition and Grenades

Some idea of the magnitude of the task is realised by the following figures :

20,000 rounds of Spigot mortar ammunition were issued, and 500 rounds for Smith Guns.

The numbers of the six types of grenades totalled 141,000.

The following weights were handed back to Ordnance :

Light   Ammunition (S.A.A. and grenades) 270 tons
Heavy   ,,   (Spigot mortar etc.)   250 ,,
Practice   ,,   50 ,,

It is computed that between 1,100 and 1,200 tons altogether were handled by Mr. Saxty and his staff, this figure includes arms, ammunition, explosives and all other equipment and stores.

BATTALION HISTORIES

Contributed By Their Commanding Officers

1ST. BATTALION WILTSHIRE HOME GUARD

THE invasion of Holland, largely by airborne troops took place on 10th May 1940. At 9 p.m. on 14th of May the then Secretary of State for War (Mr. Eden) broadcast an appeal for volunteers to be called " Local Defence Volunteers ". They were instructed to report at their nearest police station. Amongst the first men at the Chippenham Station was Mr. G. Larkham, landlord of The Little George Inn and Capt. C. S. Williams, M.C., of Westinghouse works. Simultaneously by telephone the first volunteer was Maj. Lysley, Chairman of the Chippenham Branch of Magistrates, who was to raise the Pewsham Platoon and command it until he retired for age. Thereafter volunteers poured in.

On 16th May Gen. Hon. Sir Francis Gathorne-Hardy, who had lately retired from Com.-in-Chf. Aldershot Command, summoned a number of persons to his home at Lockeridge and informed them that he had been empowered to raise Local Defence Volunteers for Wiltshire. He had decided to divide the county into about ten parts or areas, making use of existing police districts which roughly corresponded with rural district areas.

The person summoned for our area was Col. Hon. C. M. Hore-Ruthven, who had recently left the Army and settled at Calne. The other persons summoned were of similar type and sincerity. At this conference maps were studied and areas decided upon, and the area commanders told to get on with the job of raising and training men as fast as possible. The atmosphere was one of great urgency and grave outlook. The main rôles of the Local Defence Volunteers were to be observation, information, prevention of sabotage and catching of spies.

On returning to Calne, Col. Hore-Ruthven decided the first task was to find suitable persons to raise companies or platoons or similar units—they were not so called at first—and to divide the area into suitable sub-areas. The division into physical sub-areas was easy, but the collecting of suitable persons was much more difficult and much the more important, as the success of recruitment, training and organization would mainly depend on having good officers. Col. Hore-Ruthven had only recently come to live in the county and therefore did not know very many local people, so the task was not simple.

As far as can be remembered on 17th May—a Friday—Col. Ruthven, Col. E. P. Awdry, M.C. then Mayor of Chippenham, and who had recently completed his command of the Wiltshire Yeomany, and Capt. E. C. Barnes, who had served most of the First World War as an artilleryman, met at the offices of Messrs. Wood and Awdry in St. Mary Street, to discuss the names of retired officers and others who might be invited to take command of the parishes—to the number of 24 in the district—and so decide, further, which of these gentlemen had the time and ability to assume command of several parishes—company commanders as they were later to become.

In arranging the sub-division of the area it was decided that such suitable company commanders as were available should be temporarily given as large an area as they could manage, so as to cover all the ground without having to find a suitable men for every village, as someone had to take charge quickly and get things started. Thus, at first, places like Box and Colerne were included under one Commander with Corsham, and Lt.-Col. Miles (late 1st Royal Dragoons) residing at Kington Langley commanded both Kington Langley and Sutton Benger.

All this took time, for apart from finding the possible commanders, the latter had the much more difficult task of sorting out the volunteers in their parishes or groups of parishes. Their records were subject to police scrutiny before they could be sworn in and the insistence of the Police on this requirement was somewhat resented by harrassed platoon commanders in the days when speed seemed the only necessity, and useful recruits were being held up. But in the light of later knowledge, it can be seen that there was, perhaps, something to be said for providing against the risk of arming the scallywag or mentally unstable.

While all this was going on, Gen. Gathorne-Hardy was given small dribbles of rifles and ammunition, a dozen, twenty, etc., and toured the county with tremendous energy, giving a few to each area, and assisting greatly with advice and information. As said above, the atmosphere was pretty hectic as it was realised that the enemy might land sabotage parties or individuals at any time, and there might be spies and Quislings even in our midst. The Dunkirk affair was taking place and matters looked precarious, though no one knew, what we now know, how very precarious they were. There was much to be done as regards recruiting meetings in town halls etc. to explain the terms of enlistment, to reassure the ardent and to urge the reluctant.

There were also urgent problems (usually mare's nests) which occupied time, of suspicious persons in key positions. One of which was a real and remarkable one and was only solved by direct action by Gen. Gaythorne-Hardy with Headquarters of Southern Command.

On the 20th May, the first area conference presided over by Col. Ruthven took place in the room on the first floor of Messrs. Wood and Awdry's offices, which was to serve for nearly five years as Battalion Headquarters, along with its normal function of providing the scene of the solemnisation of matrimony by the Registrar, to the mutual embarrassment of all parties. This meeting was succeeded by two more on the 21st May, at Verne Leaze, Calne, and on the 22nd May, at Chippenham, which were attended by some or all of the following :

Col. The Hon. Malise Hore-Ruthven, C.M.G., D.S.O. (in command)

Maj. The Hon. R. A. Addington, Highway Manor, Calne.
Maj. C. F. Clarke, Rudloe Park, Box.
Capt. A. A. Oxford, M.C., 73 Malmesbury Road, Chippenham. (deputising for Brig. C. R. B. Carrington, D.S.O., then in hospital).
Lt.-Col. W. T. Miles, M.C., Manor House, Kington Langley.
Capt. Russell Wood, Lanhill, Chippenham.
Lt. Maurice, Castle Combe.
Capt. E. C. Barnes, Acting Adjutant.
The following is a copy of the order subsequently issued. (It should be noted that in its first paragraph the word " arranged " is used, NOT " ordered ".)

Calne and Chippenham District L.D.V.

At two meetings at Chippenham and Calne on the 20th and 21st May, the following was arranged :

The volunteers of this district will be known as a company. The number of platoons or sections in the company is unlimited, and their strength may vary. Their commanders will be known as platoon or section leaders, under sub-district commanders.

The duties are as follows :

1. *Information.* The areas must be watched, especially at dusk and dawn. All available means—runners, motor cyclists, etc., to be used, to pass on news.
2. To deal with parachutists, if possible. If not possible to be watched and information sent.
3. Blocking roads by armed parties and solid obstacles.

Reserve. All spare men to be kept as reserves to be sent where required. The towns of Chippenham, Calne and Corsham especially should retain men in reserve, and arrange for transport for them to be available.

———————————

At a meeting of the sub-district commanders held at the offices of Messrs. W. J. and D. Awdry, Chippenham on 22nd May, the following was arranged : The list o the sub-district commanders was finally settled.

The following orders were given by the Officer Commanding :
(1) Rifles and ammunition to be issued to sub-districts, as shown in the enclosed list.
(2) These rifles are to be stored or issued at discretion of sub-district commander.
(3) Officers and men in possession of uniform to wear same when on duty with armed troops.
(4) Firearms not to be carried except by men in uniform. (Note : A military cap constitutes a uniform within Geneva Convention.)
(5) Shotguns shall not be used. Sporting rifles may only be used if loaded with solid ammunition.

Observation posts to be manned as soon as personnel is available during the following hours : 9-11 p.m. and 3.30-5.30 a.m. Not less than three men to each post.

Enemy movements to be reported by leader at each post. First to Police ; secondly to his immediate superior.

Sub-district commanders to find out from their own telephone exchanges how best to communicate with appropriate police and to establish liaison as soon as may be with adjoining districts or sub-districts.

A number of other points were left over for decision by higher authority.

Before going on into details of how the duties and orders given above were carried out, the following comments may be of interest.

The term sub-district has now appeared in an order dated 23rd May 40 in addition to that of sub-area, and in it we see mention too of a section leader (Note : leader not commander). The fact was that at this stage in the proceedings, authority was inspired by the desire to avoid all military titles, whether on grounds of democratic equality (which was highly probable) or to avoid the risk of undue weight being attached to the views or appearance of distinguished soldiers of Boer War or earlier campaigns, is not known. But, while this order authorised the wearing of uniform by those who had it, another, published shortly afterwards, forbade the wearing of insignia of rank. It is on record that soon afterwards the " Area " Commander (i.e. Gen. Gathorne-Hardy) appeared in Battalion Headquarters with nothing on his shoulder straps but red collar tabs still in position, saying that he had wired to the War Office to expostulate. At the same time it was made clear that any Local Defence Volunteer, however exalted, would be subordinate in action to any other regular officer, however junior. " Very well," said the General grimly, " but I shall give the young gentleman on the road block outside my house plenty of good advice."

It is interesting to observe the exclusive reliance on Police channels for communications. At this very early stage there was virually no liason between the Local Defence Volunteers and the Army. Was there indeed any Army with which to liaise ? The B.E.F. were still in France and did not much look like getting out of it.

Then road-blocks. We mostly patrolled at their early stage. What road-blocks there were, were formed by wagons—carts drawn across the road (we had blocks by dozens later—about every mile). These were not the most convenient obstructions to remove for the passage of legitimate traffic nor were they always well lit. A ten ton milk lorry and trailer coming too fast down Derry Hill collided at the bottom with the Pewsham obstruction, which happened to be one of Maj. Lysley's hay wagons. The wagon went for six—it was wanted for hay-making next day—the lorry overturned, rivers of milk flowed down the hill—but no one was hurt.

Finally arms. In original orders it does not appear quite clear whether shotguns were contrary to the Geneva Convention, anyway, it is certain that owners of them had been asked to leave them on loan at police stations and many valuable guns had been forthcoming. Capt. Barnes has clear recollection of waiting for the foe in the early dawn with an armament better suited to scare a flight of duck. It is certain too that on tour of inspection in the dark, Col. Ruthven was to learn only too well, what it felt like to have a twelve-bore pressed to the pit of his stomach by a zealous volunteer quite oblivious of the refinements of a safety catch.

A few—a very few rifles—good Lee-Enfield ·303s were issued with ten rounds to each and strict orders not to fire them off except in action. That was on May 24th. These were to be left under lock and key. The habits made by 300 years of peace in England were not to be discarded overnight and it was only after years of war that a loaded tommy-gun became a normal part of the furniture of cottage or farm-house.

S.D. caps, arm bands and rifles were very few in number, and on many occasions it was necessary for men to wait their turn for some of these valuable articles before they were qualified to proceed on duty. From a record dated 18th June 40 the Battalion's night duty entailed :

10 O.P.s with patrols
37 road-blocks

Men enrolled and awaiting enrolment was then 2,139 with 165 rifles. The number of shotguns is recorded at 370, most of these were privately owned.

Many rules were laid down about road-blocks and the method of halting and challenging vehicles. Red lanterns had to be displayed in some way or another. Higher authority thought it was a somewhat risky job for a sentry to hold and swing a red lantern to the oncoming vehicle, partly because, if an enemy, he might not choose to stop, and also, if he did, he would know whereabouts to aim his tommy-gun. It was therefore ordered that the red lantern should be suspended on a tripod or some such way, and that a string should be attached to it, the other end of which would be held by the sentry secreted in the hedge or ditch, who on the approach of a car would pull the string in such a manner as to make the inmates of the vehicle think it was being swung by hand. It is feared that this order was never taken very seriously.

Maj. Williams, M.C., who commanded the Home Guard at Chippenham practically throughout their existence, tells a story of when, in a fit of energy, he took a tour of his various posts (as a matter of fact he never missed his turn on the duty roster). On approaching one post and being challenged he answered " Visiting rounds." The sentry, who provided milk in the neighbourhood, replied, " Advance visiting rounds, I know you as being one of my customers."

About the beginning of July 1940, Col. Hore-Ruthven was appointed to a training brigade in Scotland, and Brig. C. R. B. Carrington, late R.A., who was then commanding the Local Defence Volunteers in Chippenham, was given command of the Battalion in which capacity he remained. Col. Hore-Ruthven returned at the beginning of 1941 and took over second in command of the Battalion and greatly contributed to the efficiency of the unit.

Capt. Barrett, late Q.M. to the Wiltshire Yeomanry, was then doing wonderful work, as clothing and stores were becoming more in evidence. It was greatly due to his former experience in quartermaster's work that the Battalion, mostly composed of civilians, was started off on the right lines, i.e. taking receipts for issues and the keeping of ledgers under the various headings as different articles turned up, etc., etc.

After a little time, the work of this department became a whole-time job, and Capt. Barrett, then over seventy years of age, was unable to give sufficient time to his own business, and as no money was at this early stage available to pay for help Capt. Barrett was compelled to give up. This was a great loss to the Battalion. Anyway, although the store (a small shed up Rowden Hill) was full of the issued equipment, stores, etc., the ledgers clearly kept by Capt. Barrett showed exactly what was in it.

All company commanders were summoned to help and came to the stores at certain times. Capt. Somerset who had commanded a section of the Local Defence Volunteers and was sixty-seven years of age, also came to the assistance and rendered invaluable service, subsequently taking on the job of Q.M. until the appointment of regular Q.M.s at the beginning of 1942. He kept on in this department until the end ; his devotion to duty in his extreme loyalty and also his never failing exertions to help everybody, no matter what trouble it was, Capt. Somerset became admired and loved by all with whom he came in contact.

The stores which contained many hundreds of haversacks, anklets, boots, caps, scabbards and bayonets (smeared in grease), some greatcoats, blouses and trousers, were all distributed, and company commanders went away satisfied that they had had a fair deal. The only mistake made was in the issue of anklets. Corsham counted theirs out in single ones instead of in pairs and consequently only got half of what they should. However, the deficiency was made up later.

The store was completely cleared with the exception of some shotguns which it had not been considered safe to issue. These were taken over by the Chippenham Company who always had an unsatiable thirst for weapons of any sort ; these guns were put in order by Mr. Jackson an artificer of the Regular Army in the last war ; he was finally promoted to lieutenant and was presented with a Com.-in-Chf.s Certificate of Merit. Jackson's work throughout was magnificent, and although really belonging to the Chippenham Company, he did the work for the whole Battalion.

The strength of the Battalion at the commencement of July 1940, with their commanders in the various localities, was as follows :

Compton Bassett Company, afterwards called " Whitehorse " and finally " A ".
Commander, Hon. Maj. R. A. Addington (late of India Horse). Remained O.C. throughout.

Platoons	Commander	Approx. no. of men	Remarks
Hilmarton	Mr. Chamings	51	Commanded throughout.
Compton Bassett	Capt. Guy Benson	41	Lt. Devening took over.
Cherhill	Mr. House	76	Lt. Ayres took over.
Calstone	Mr. Maundrell	40	Commanded throughout.
Heddington	Mr. Perrett	32	,, ,,
Pewsham	Major Lysley (late of Yeomanry)	114	Retired for age. Lt. Palmer took over.

Company Total **354**

Calne Company, finally known as " B " Company.
Commander, Capt. M. E. Cook, M.C. (late R.A.). Remained O.C. throughout.

Platoons	*Commander*	*Approx. no. of men*	*Remarks*
Northern	Mr. R. T. Harris	67	Lt. A. G. L. Good took over May 1942.
Centre	Mr. C. G. Higgens	91	Commanded throughout.
Southern	C. H. Batch (late India Horse)	60	Lt. Rawkins took over until succeeded by Lt. E. J. Beynon, 1st Oct. 1943, and subsequently by Lt. S. A. Marsh, 2nd Dec. 1943.
Harris Bacon Factory		30	

Company Total 248

Corsham Company, after designated as " C " Company.
Commander, Lt.-Col. Waterworth, then Maj. Pay and finally Maj. Skrine, M.C.

Platoons	*Commander*	*Approx. no. of men*	*Remarks*
Lacock	Lt.-Col. Jackson (late R.A.)	76	Commanded throughout.
Hartham	Mr. Tucker	15	,, ,,
Gastard	Capt. Harris	44	Lt. Gale succeeded in 1942 and retained command onwards.
Neston	Col. Fuller (late of Wiltshire Yeomanry and 75 years old)	53	Fuller retired for age. Mr. N. Stainer took over, and in 1944 was succeeded by Lt. The Hon. A. Methuen.
Corsham and Pickwick	Capt. Harris	82	Followed by Maj. Pay, then Lt. Curry, and finally by Lt. Gough.

Company Total 270

Box and Colerne Company, finally designated as " D " Company.

Commander, Maj. Morley (late Wiltshire Yeomanry) commanded throughout.
Assisted in the beginning by Maj. Wade, late K.O.S.B.s.

Platoon	*Commander*	*Approx. no. of men*	*Remarks*
Box Village (divided into four sections)	Mr. W. Martin	89	Capt. Skrine, M.C., took over shortly after until March 1943.
Ditteridge	Mr. F. Goulstone	35	All of these were finally merged into one platoon under Capt. Skrine. Mr. Henderson took over, then Mr. Thompson, succeeded by Henderson and kept command until his death in December 1944.
Kingsdown	Mr. H. D. Ancell	24	
Wadswick	Mr. B. W. Gibbon	18	
Colerne	Mr. F. Bedford. Assisted by Mr. W. Thompson, late of R.A.F.	122	

Company Total 288

Chippenham Company, finally designated " E " Company.

Commander : Capt. Oxford started it off until Brig. C. R. B. Carrington arrived in the beginning of June 1940. He commanded for a month, and then handed over to Capt. C. S. Williams, M.C., who very ably carried on throughout the remaining period.

Platoon	*Commander*	*Approx. no. of men*	*Remarks*
No. 1 (S.E. Section)	Mr. S. Perry		Early taken over by Mr. C. M. Townsend to the end.
No. 2 (W. Section)	Mr. Northover	*Company Total* 532	Early taken over by Mr. Hawser.
No. 3 (N.W. Section)	Mr. Wentworth		Early taken over by Mr. C. B. Jamieson to end.
No. 4 (N.E. Section)	Mr. J. Price		About May 1942 Lt. Sheard took over to end.
Westinghouse Block	Capt. C. S. Williams, M.C.		1st July 1940 Capt. Williams took over command of the whole company when it was reorganised.

Fossway Company, finally designated " F ".
Commander, Capt. Russell Wood. Soon after taken over by Maj. Allen who commanded to the end.

Platoon	Commander	Approx. no. of men	Remarks
Chippenham Without	Capt. Somerset	14	Finally merged into Langley Burrell.
Biddestone	Mr. Gunton	40	Taken over in 1943 by Mr. Travers.
North Wraxall	Mr. Clark	40	Commanded to end.
Ford and Slaughterford	Mr. Pearce	28	,, ,, ,,
Burton and West Kington	Mr. Brown	54	,, ,, ,,
Grittleton	Mr. Harding	41	,, ,, ,,
Littleton Drew	?	27	Taken over by Mr. Slade in end of 1942.
Castle Combe	Lt. Maurice	37	
Yatton Keynell	Mr. Blythe	39	Commanded to end.

Company Total 320

Kington Langley Company, finally designated as " G " Company.
Commander, Lt.-Col. Miles, M.C., late O.C. 1st Royal Dragoons until his death in 1943. Capt. Soames then took over to the end.

Platoon	Commander	Approx. no. of men	Remarks
Kington St. Michael	Maj. Malcom Thompson	44	Taken over by Lt. Soames in 1942 when Maj. Thompson went as Second in Command, Company.
Kington Langley	Maj. Phillips	46	Followed by Mr. Kendzior, then Mr. Reeves to end.
Langley Burrell	Capt. Reid (late R.A.)	32	Followed by Mr. Fairclough then Mr. Short to the end.
Stanton	Mr. H. Jones	30	Followed by his son to end.

Company Total 152

Sutton Benger Company, subsequently designated " H " Company.

Commander, Lt.-Col. Fishe, D.S.O., late R.A. Followed in Jan. 1941 by Maj. M. S. D. Day, M.C., who most ably commanded the Company to the end.

Platoon	Commander	Approx. no. of men	Remarks
Bremhill	Mr. Clive Hillier	40	Commanded an excellent platoon throughout.
Foxham	Mr. E. A. Bryning	32	Beginning of 1941, Mr. R. V. Pegler took over command, to the end.
Christian Malford	Mr. A. Heale	48	After a few weeks, Mr. H. Gold took over until Sept. 1943, when Lt. Woodcock carried on to the end.
East Tytherton and Spirthill	Mr. R. S. Baker	32	Retired for age Jan. 1942 and was succeeded by Lt. F. E. Birtell who commanded to the end.
Sutton Benger and Draycot	Rev. E. A. Newberry	50	Retired in May 1942 and succeeded by Mr. M. H. Hughes who carried on to the end.

Company Total 202

The total strength of the Battalion at the beginning of July 1940 was approximately 2,300. This rose within the next few months to over 2,400. It then gradually diminished until compulsory service was introduced in 1942. The ceiling of the Battalion was given at 3,100 but this was never reached. The highest recorded was approximately 2,800 ; this was the strength, which with slight fluctuation, remained to the end. The fact that the ceiling was never reached can be attributed to the " call-up " to the Regular Forces of the younger members, being about equal to those freshly enrolled in the Home Guard.

Training. It can be said with some certainty that the backbone of the Home Guard from start to finish was the members who had had previous service with the Army ; besides this, there were in each sub-unit " enthusiasts " who learnt quickly and never missed a parade.

The cry for instructors was general ; throughout the Battalion area, classes to teach rifle drill, etc., were started in the early days—one in Chippenham by Lt.-Col. E. Awdry (late of Wiltshire Yeomanry) at his private house, 12 Rowden Hill and the other by Mr. Larkham at The Little George Inn (of which he was then proprietor, and also late P.S.I. to the 4th Wiltshires). This ex-regular was re-enlisted in 1942 and became one of the Battalion P.S.I.s. It is only to be regretted that Mr. Larkham was not so appointed earlier, for he proved himself invaluable as well as indefatigable, and by his reliability, calmness, tact and loyalty, became universally popular and respected by all. He attended many courses, thus keeping himself well up with the various weapons allotted to the Home Guard from time to time.

Sgt.-Maj. Rutty, was also an excellent P.S.I. and it can be said with confidence that he contributed very materially to the efficiency of the Battalion. He was also very popular and kept himself up to date.

The Battalion's third P.S.I. was Sgt.-Maj. Goodenough. He was young, but despite this he got on with some of the units, although he required considerably more experience.

A certain amount of marching drill was necessary. This was necessarily somewhat resented by those with previous service, and there is no doubt it was indulged in to excess by those instructors who did not feel themselves sufficiently competent to teach other soldier-like activities. Some Local Defence Volunteers were quite touchy, should reference be made as regards their stature when forming up on parade. A story is told of one rather short and portly member, when relegated to the rear rank, straightway handed in his cap and armlet and never appeared again.

As time wore on, instructors came from regular troops in the neighbourhood, and others further afield. Capt. Dodgson from Royal Tank Corps at Tidworth, which formed part of the striking force due to come to the assistance in the Battalion area, should " action stations " be ordered, was very helpful, and brought over P.T. instructors to teach unarmed combat and other methods of fighting that it was considered suitable for the Local Defence Volunteers to know and practice on Hitler's invasion troops. The Rev. Palmer, later O.C. Pewsham Platoon, although not a big man was amongst the best in the class. Capt. Dodgson, besides holding cadre classes for the Battalion, visited companies and individual platoons. In addition, he arranged rifle practice, demonstrations with tanks and the methods of warfare, also inspections by large parties of the Battalion at Tidworth ; besides this, meals, etc., were arranged, and everyone was most hospitably received.

Another very helpful person was Col. Chity, who with his regiment, the West Kents, encamped near Rudloe was always ready to send instructors anywhere at any time, to say nothing of arranging a battle. These were always full of dash, and as near the real thing, without bullets, as could be. At one battle with the Box Platoon, Bren carriers, motor cyclists, lorries, bricks, stones and clods of earth were flying in every direction. A lorry was seen to deliberately turn across the path of a motor cyclist travelling at about forty miles per hour. The result was that the motor cyclist came heavily to grief on the pavement and was picked up in a considerably dazed and shaky condition ; the lorry driver said they were to act in this way during exercises. The Colonel was informed of the accident but only enquired whether the " motor cycle " was all right. He was a popular C.O. but the members of the regiment complained that he expected them all to be V.C.s. Anyway they taught Box Platoon a lot, and their departure for the Isle of Wight, was a sad blow.

Courses at the Local Defence Volunteer School, Osterly, were attended, the first to go being Capt. Williams, M.C., of Chippenham. As far as is remembered they lasted from Fridays to Mondays and Tuesdays to Thursdays. Although not very long, they were very strenuous and the accommodation and feeding, did not in any way resemble comfort or make you think you had eaten too much. However the lessons taught were good and Capt. Williams wrote an excellent resume of the course of which he had copies made for circulation throughout the Battalion. Later the School moved to Denbies, near Dorking, where general conditions were somewhat improved. Several officers and men attended.

Mr. Langdon Davis, an expert on fighting in Spain, etc., gave a lecture in the Gaumont Cinema at Chippenham early in 1941, to about 1,200 of the Battalion.

A weak spot in the Home Guard was the junior N.C.O.s and for these cadre classes run by Battalion in addition to companies, were found to be most beneficial.

Bombs and their throwing, started in the early days. " Molotov Cocktails " which consisted of a bottle, any size, preferably one pint capacity, partly filled with petrol and partly tar, with a rag steeped in petrol. When lighted, the conents of the bottle broke when thrown on the tank, and ignited the same, the burning liquid going into the cracks of the tank or causing so much heat outside as to scorch or otherwise inconvenience the inmates. Anyway, they had been proved effective and Capt. Benson of Compton Bassett, gave a very able demonstration in their construction and effect, when ignited. The warming of the tar before it was put into the bottle, appeared to be one of the tips when filling.

Battalion courses were held on bombs of all sorts with which the Home Guard were issued. This entailed the teaching of their contents and practical work of throwing live grenades. Examinations were held and those reaching a certain standard were deemed to be qualified as instructors in live grenades.

In the early days when No. 36 grenades were issued, instructors with sufficient experience in the priming and throwing of these bombs were few. Sgt. Pritchard of Corsham Company, who served with the Guards in the 1914 War, volunteered to go anywhere in the Battalion area to give instruction on live grenades. In a quarry near Biddestone where he was instructing, one of the learners failed to throw his bomb over the parapet. The bomb lodged half-way down the slope and Sgt. Pritchard, regardless of personal danger, extricated the grenade from behind a stone and threw it to safety, thereby saving casualties which would probably have been fatal. For this act of bravery, he was recommended for award, and it was not until after many years had passed and the Home Guard " Stood Down ", that he was awarded a Com.-in-Chf.s Certificate of Merit.

On 4th May, 1941, the Battalion organised a competition in the Chippenham Sports Grounds for the throwing of Molotov and No. 36 grenades. Each company could enter one team of six from one section. The same pit was used, but the places from which the bombs were thrown were changed, so as to bring out the various methods and conditions in which a bomb might have to be thrown. Regular

36

forces provided the judges. The competition was a success and was won by a section of Cherhill Platoon of Whitehorse Company (" A ").

Later on several Battalion competitions were organised ; one for Lewis Guns, Blacker Bombards and Northover teams. On 4th October 1942, " C " Company won with the highest aggregate for all three weapons. The last of such competitions involved every weapon that had been issued to the Home Guard, with the exception of the 60-pounder and 2-pounder anti-tank guns. These competitions took place on 8th October, 15th October and 22nd October 1944 and the results were :

Rifle	Competition won by	Lacock Platoon, " C " Company
Smith Gun	,, ,, ,,	Foxham Platoon, " H " Company
Grenade	,, ,, ,,	Calstone Platoon, " A " Company
Sten Gun	,, ,, ,,	H.Q. Platoon, " B " Company
Spigot Mortar	,, ,, ,,	Heddington Platoon, " A " Company.
Lewis Gun	,, ,, ,,	Northern Platoon, " B " Company
B.A. Rifle	,, ,, ,,	Centre Platoon, " B " Company.
B.M. Gun	,, ,, ,,	" W " Battle Platoon, " E " Company.
E.Y. Rifle	,, ,, ,,	Gastard Platoon, " C " Company.

All such competitions meant that the teams had, first, to have won eliminating competitions within their companies, and in 1944, this helped greatly to keep up some enthusiasm, especially after the invasion of the Continent was successfully established.

In December 1942, the Battalion was issued with two 60-pounder guns. One was taken on by Chippenham and the other by Calne. Lt. Kershaw at Chippenham, took to gunnery like a duck to water, and soon mastered the art of indirect fire and predicted shooting, besides training a complete detachment for the gun. Maj. Cook, Officer Commanding, Calne Company (late Horse Artillery gunner), was very keen and soon raised and trained a detachment.

Both guns were taken up at different times by road to Larkhill and fired with excellent results. Lt. Kershaw worked out his predicted shoot so well, that his first shot was only about 100x—at a range of 8,000. The staff at Larkhill were very helpful to say nothing of the help given in accommodation, etc., by the 4th Field Training Regiment to whom nothing ever appeared too much trouble.

Many T.E.W.T.S. were organised by Battalion Headquarters, both for officers and prospective commanders. Col. Burn, O.C. Troops, Corsham, who was finally in direct command of all Home Guard in the Western Sector of Wiltshire, always attended any sort of exercise that was going on, no matter how trivial, providing his other commitments, which were very numerous, allowed ; his extreme good nature, common sense and humane understanding, made him admired and loved by all.

Capt. R. P. Boulton of the 4th Battalion Wiltshire Regiment, was appointed as adjutant to the Battalion, in January 1942. As all administrative work was at this time being very successfully done by Maj. Wade, who, on his return from the R.A.F., took up the post of administration officer from Capt. E. C. Barnes. This latter officer had had the job from the start and right well he did it. His work was very greatly appreciated by the O.C.s companies and without his help and organising abilities, they could not have hoped to carry on.

It was decided that the new adjutant should concentrate his abilities on training and courses generally. It was a big task at which he did his best, and was generally popular.

In October 1942 battle drill was instituted for the Home Guard. This was at first greeted with very mixed feelings, but after the initial stages, it was accepted as a great innovation in training. Battle drill combined with field training and also with battle innoculation formed the culminating types of training. These were practiced chiefly at " Kents Bottom ", a deep valley running between Yatton Keynell and West Dean ; this valley was a scene of many activities including the firing of spigot mortars, grenade throwing, etc.

Rifle ranges were not plentiful in early days. Kings Play (above Calstone) and Box ranges were the only ones which it was practical for the Battalion to use. There was a limited ration of ammunition allowed for practice, and the general complaint was that practically no shooting was being carried out. In Westmeads, Chippenham, a rifle range had once existed but the target gallery and stop - butt had disappeared ; however, with the aid of the Borough Surveyor (Mr. Phillips), two targets were let into the bank on the river bend, the bullets being stopped (at any rate a certain number of them) by the sloping bank in the rear. These targets were engaged at ranges up to 200x, as this was then considered the limit of range at which the Local Defence Volunteers should open fire, thereby saving ammunition by killing their bird every time. This range, although primative, proved of value, and the members of the Chippenham Company made good use of it while evenings were light enough to see.

Maj. Day, M.C., O.C. Sutton Benger Company (" H "), a very keen and enthusiastic officer who always had a way either round or over difficulties, made a range on the old Dauntsey-Malmesbury railway track, using an old bridge over the track as a stop-butt. It was a great help to his company and no complaints were received of stray bullets.

Another range at Duncombe Bottom near " The Shoe ", N. Wraxall and belonging to the R.A.F. at Colerne was also used by the Home Guard out in that direction ; it was not a good range but was *better than nothing*.

In April 1943 when the regular troops had left, Cowage Farm (Near Calne), Bowden Park (above Lacock), Pool Farm (Biddestone), Lanhill and Draycot House were taken over the the Battalion and allotted to the various companies for week-end camps. In the Park at Draycot, a field firing range was incorporated and used both by " E " and " H " Companies at their week-end camps.

" B " Company who used Bowden Park were able, by kind permission of Capt. F. Spicer, to use some ground in Spy Park where it was possible to practice some field firing during the year 1943. 1,542 officers and other ranks attended week-end camps.

In 1944 certain searchlight sites were taken over ; the one at Calstone proved especially valuable, and was used for Battalion training camps and also by companies. In all cases, rations were purchased and issued by the Supplies Platoon of this battalion's H.Q. company, of which Lt. Wright was the commander ;j his civilian knowledge (manager of Wilts. Bacon Co.) of catering, etc., was an absolute godsend, and the whole of the arrangements for cooking, messing and general duties were undertaken by this H.Q. platoon.

Maj. Hon. R. A. Addington, Commander of " A " Company, very kindly put up a silver challenge cup and medals for the winner and runner-up for the best all round man at arms in the Battalion. This consisted of rifle shooting, 36, 74 and grenades including tests and general knowledge, also bayonet fighting over a course in which marks were given for " elan ", " determination and controlled fury ", etc. This took place during November 1944 and was won by Corp. G. W. Green of " B " Company, scoring 244 marks out of a possible 300 in the rifle shooting. This cup is now competed for by the best shot on the open range of the rifle clubs (ten in all) belonging or formed in Battalion area and it was won in 1945 by Sgt.-Maj. Larkham who shot as a member of Kington Langley Rifle Club.

In the Battalion H.Q. company (which originally consisted of three members and ended up with a strength over a hundred), besides the supplies section there were :

> Signal Section, under the command of Lt. Hunt.
> Intelligence Section, under the command of Lt. Burdge.
> Transport Section, under the command of Lt. Dyke.
> Security and General Duty, under the command of Sgt. Perry.

The whole of the above specialised watertight departments were under the command of Capt. Wayte Smith.

Lt. Hunt originally raised a signal section in the Chippenham Company at which he proved himself an expert, and when it came to forming a Battalion H.Q. section, Maj. Williams of " E " Company, very kindly allowed (and Hunt consented) to take it on. He worked very hard and got personnel together, and in the end the general efficiency was equal to any Regular Army unit. The chief call was for wireless sets ; a few were issued with ranges up to about three miles. This was not long enough as the Battalion area was about twenty miles long and in some places ten miles broad. Pigeons were also organised and used at some exercises. Mr. Vickery of the G.W.R. gave great assistance in supplying the birds. At one time special classes for handling pigeons were got up.

In May 1942, it was decided to start an intelligence branch throughout the Battalion, and Sgt. Burdge of No. 4 Platoon, " E " Company, was asked to take the job on. Burdge agreed and with the aid of Sgt. Wheeler also from No. 4 Platoon, " E " Company, got started. Burdge attended short courses. An " I " officer or N.C.O. was required from each company who, in their turn, had to raise an " I " man in each platoon. This was somewhat resented at first as it probably meant the platoon commander placing another good man in a new job, for at this time, what with Northovers, spigot mortars, Lewis Guns, signallers and various specialist teams of this sort, those left to form the battle drill platoon were gradually dwindling to a dangerous minimum. However the whole team of " I " men was finally completed. Weekly meetings of company " I " officers and N.C.O.s were held at Chippenham and each company " I " man took a pride in presenting a report of work done in his company ; this method of self-teaching proved very successful. Pte. Emery was added to the strength of the Battalion " I " section.

Great praise is due to Lt. Burdge and Lt. Wheeler for all the excellent work they did and for the very satisfactory results obtained.

The rôle of the Home Guard varied from time to time. Road-blocks, patrols, O.P.s, defended villages, check points, tank islands, centres of resistance, etc., etc., to the final stage of mobility, leaving a few to make a nuisance at bottleneck road centres.

The Home Guard at Chippenham—850 strong—complete with battery of 6 Smith Guns, and at Calne—250 strong—also with some artillery, were finally allotted the rôle of a sort of " striking force ", mobile with ear-marked transport (lorries and bicycles) to move anywhere in the Battalion area. Some exercises to this end were practiced with success.

Other companies were partly mobile with the exception of " H " Company who were practically completely mobile.

A calling-up alarm for " action stations " was sometimes laid on, the record of " all on parade " in fifty minutes, for a rural area, was not very much above the average. Once in the first year of the Local Defence Volunteers' existence, a certain code word was to be given for " action stations " should the Germans invade. One company commander, who always affirmed that this event was not possible and would never take place, was rung up in the early hours and given the code word (which had been received from higher authority), as Germans were reported to have landed not far from Bristol. This company commander's only remark was a small word in the plural beginning with " B ", and as the story goes, went straight back to bed and so to sleep peacefully until his usual time in the morning. When morning came, the report of hostile landing had proved false and one company, at any rate, had been thus spared a disturbed night.

At the third and fourth anniversary of the Home Guard, demonstrations were held throughout the Battalion area, the chief ones being at Chippenham, Calne and Corsham. A big parade and march past were arranged in Chippenham followed by a display in Monkton Park of arms and an attack on a farm-house occupied by Germans ; after being blown to pieces by careful timing of exploding concealed mines, which represented explosions from spigot mortar bombs, which was arranged admirably by Lt. Bushnell, the house burst into flames and a charge of attacking troops went in and led the captured prisoners, who were in German uniform back for the audience to admire. A collection was made at the gate, £60 being raised for the Wiltshire Regiment P.O.W. Funds. Capt's Townsend and Cadman deserved great praise for their excellent stage management of these demonstrations.

Calne and Corsham had similar displays ; most villages putting up a display of a battle platoon in action and a show of the various weapons in their possession.

In 1943 the Battalion received about ninety personnel who worked for the Admiralty Underground Works near Pickwick. These were finally formed into

" J " Company under Maj. Lambert and were issued with nine 20 m.m. Hispano Guns on anti-aircraft mountings. They came under A.A. Command for training and operational duties, but were administered by this Battalion. They were very kind and obliging, often putting lorries at the disposal of the Battalion Q.M. department, when it was at a loss for other transport. This company under its able commander became an efficient unit and was allowed to wear the A.A. arm badge on their battle dress, and so proud were they of this, that even on very cold days, they preferred to suffer from the climatic conditions sooner than cover up their badge with a greatcoat.

A word here must be said of " E " Company of Chippenham. This company was always over 500 strong and after conscription had come into force its number rose to over 850 and had a ceiling of 1,000. On several occasions it was suggested by Salisbury Plain District that it should become an independent battalion, but its commander, Maj. Williams, M.C., preferred to remain as part of the old Battalion, saying he had not the time to spend running about to conferences and demonstrations, etc., at the same time indicating that he would rather serve under the command of the devil he knew, rather than one he was not certain of ; needless to say the O.C. 1st Battalion Wiltshire Home Guard gladly accepted Maj. Williams' verdict and felt greatly honoured by the non-acceptance of the promotion offered them. Maj. Williams, however, organised the company more or less on a battalion basis. It finally consisted of, in addition to an excellent band, four infantry companies, called " battle companies " and each commanded by captains ; one artillery troop consisting of 60-pounder Smith Guns and 2-pounder anti-tank guns ; one signal section ; one bomb disposal squad. This auxiliary bomb disposal unit was trained and commanded by Capt. C. R. Lewis, who did this in addition to his other Home Guard work of administration officer to the company. This unit was remarkably good, and considering the small amount of training that was possible with their exceptionally long hours of civilian work, it was felt certain the members would not have failed in their duty had circumstances demanded their services.

It would have been a very great loss to the Battalion, had " E " Company become a battalion on its own. They were at all times ready to help anybody when in difficulties, especially when specialists were required to swell the Battalion H.Q. staff ; it was largely due to Maj. Williams' unselfish generosity and broadmindedness in transferring some of his best men, that Battalion H.Q. became, it is hoped, an efficient administrating unit.

" H " Company under the command of Maj. Day, M.C., could be said to specialise in mobility ; with the exception of the Christian Malford and Sutton Benger Platoons, whose rôle for some time held them more or less static to the Avon Bridge and five-arch railway bridge in their areas, its others at Bremhill, Foxham, East Tytherton, mostly farmers and their employees, raised enough cars and cattle floats to move them with the greatest rapidity in any direction when paratroops had been spotted to land. On exercises, exceptionally high m.p.h. in the narrow and twisty roads were attained and any umpire or other such unimportant person would do well to keep in the ditch for safety. Very keen competition ensued, and Maj. Day and all concerned must be congratulated on the results their unceasing efforts attained.

Subsistance allowance at the rate of 1/6 per five hours on Local Defence Volunteer duty away from home, was brought into being in August 1940. This allowance owing to the general spirit of national economy, was not claimed by many at first. It was on a very hot day later, at the termination of an exercise involving about a hundred Local Defence Volunteers that it was claimed. After the conference at which Col. Congreve from H.Q., Salisbury Plain District was present, and the troops had assembled, it happened that the White Hart public house at Ford Village was in the immediate vicinity, the O.C. Battalion, at the end of the conference, noticing that many Local Defence Volunteers looked very hot and thirsty, mentioned that he regretted his purse would not allow for providing refreshment for all, whereupon Col. Congreve remarked, why not use the subsistence allowance? This was enough, so the C.O., calculating it would be at least five hours' duty by the time most of the members reached their homes again, ordered a pint or its equivalent all round, the charge for which the proprietor was instructed to send to Battalion H.Q. The account duly arrived, charging for 100 pints of beer, and as it was thought that difficulty might be experienced with the auditors at Territorial Army Association if put so definitely, the landlord was asked to submit a new account and call it " refreshments " in lieu of " beer ". It was passed and paid O.K. This was the first time subsistence allowance was drawn in the Battalion ; afterwards it became a common practice and all pickets, guards, etc drew it. Some platoons pooled the money drawn and should any balance be over after providing the necessary food for the guard, it was put to reserve and in some cases, greatly assisted a good meal later on, when all could enjoy it together.

An A. & Q. duties officer was appointed to the Battalion on 29th May 1942. His name was Maj. Newington and he had been recently employed at Southern Command H.Q., Salisbury. On joining, he told the Battalion C.O. that he considered his duty to be such that he would relieve him of all responsibility of any work outside the actual training of the Battalion, for its operational duty and matters directly appertaining thereto. This he nobly did and as the time went on the Battalion became more and more regularised with arms and equipment of all sorts, also more and more returns, etc., were called for from higher authority. The A. & Q. officer had enough, if not more than enough, to do. He organised the Home Guard staff in such a way, that no matter whether it was a week-end camp or a battle, everything seemed made to " wind up ". Companies complained somewhat of the paper war he was apt to produce, but despite this, they well knew his efficiency and that if they wanted anything he was the person to go to in their trouble. When the end came, his organisation for the withdrawal and collection of stores, weapons, etc. proved more than satisfactory and worked like clockwork. Besides his ordinary work, he always was ready to help umpire or perform other tasks which affected training.

The Battalion Accounts came under his direction, and Mr. Hunter was employed to do them; these accounts were always an infernal nuisance. The obtaining of receipts from individuals out in remote platoon districts, from men who were *never* " in " when their houses were visited, made rendering of the accounts a very considerable job and one, which a hard-worked farmer or business man as a platoon commander, could ill afford, to the other Home Guard duties he was expected to perform in his spare moments. Major Addington of " A " Company proposed that a field cashier should go round and pay all bills and allowances with cash on the spot, but had there been one of these such officials appointed to each battalion, it is quite certain he would have only got half-way round, when it was time to start again.

The Battalion monthly accounts amounted in the latter stages of the Home Guard to some £600. Thanks to Mr. Hunter's experience in keeping accounts and his co-operation with all accounts, only a very small adverse balance remained, when they were finally closed.

There were seven doctors in the Battalion, Maj. T. Briscoe being the senior medical officer. All did very good work, especially Dr. James at Calne, whose company there had, thanks to him, a most efficient organisation.

The Battalion total armament at the " Stand Down " of the Home Guard was : 2 60-pounder guns, 4 2-pounder anti-tank guns, 14 Smith Guns and trailers, 56 Spigot mortars, 27 Northovers, 10 Browning Automatic Rifles, 33 Lewis machine-guns, 3 Browning machine-guns, 5 Vickers machine-guns, 662 Sten guns, 1,395 ·300 rifles including 106 fitted with E.Y.s, 9 20 m.m. Hispano Guns and 60 ·22 rifles.

On the 3rd December 1944, the " Stand Down " Parade took place in John Cole's Park, Chippenham, at which some 1,400 members of the Battalion took part. It was a cold and damp day which it is thought somewhat affected the numbers. The band of the R.A.O.C. from Corsham led the parade in its subsequent march past.

The O.C. Battalion read out the messages from the King and General H. E. Franklyn, Com.-in-Chf. Home Forces, to the Home Guard. He then addressed the Battalion, pointing out their achievements and thanking them for their loyalty and service they had rendered in the national cause. General Sir Alexander Godley, G.C.B., D.S.O., then arrived, and after thanking them for the part they had played, and their magnificent contribution towards bringing the war to a successful end, he proceeded to the Town Hall where he was joined by the Mayor and Corporation. General Godley then took the salute as the Battalion marched by on the way to its final dismissal.

On the 13th December 1944, about 120 officers of the Battalion attended a dinner in the Drill Hall. Lt. Wright of H.Q. Supplies Section very nobly took on the responsibility of the catering and general arrangements. A band from Calne provided music during the evening. Most sub-units held their own dinners which were all accompanied by some vocal and musical entertainment ; all were considered very successful and the probability of yearly or bi-yearly reunions were very much in evidence. It was generally agreed that the Home Guard had brought about a comradeship which otherwise might have lain dormant ; many friendships were made between those who might never have met.

The following award and Com.-in-Chf. Certificates of Merit were given to members of the Battalion as under :

B.E.M.

Sgt. F. W. Hood	" E " Coy.		Sgt. F. W. Hood	" E " Coy.
			Sgt. F. E. Hulbert	" E " Coy.
			S/Sgt. W. J. Jackson	" E " Coy.
Com.-in-Chf. Certificates			Sgt. J. R. Jefferies	" C " Coy.
Capt. F. Berryman	" E " Coy.		C.Q.M.S. G. H. King	" G " Coy.
Sgt. F. W. E. Clark	" E " Coy.		Sgt. M. Mason	" B " Coy.
Maj. M. E. Cook, M.C.	" B " Coy.		Sgt. F. Merritt	" A " Coy.
Sgt. F. Dutton	" B " Coy.		Sgt. J. Neate	" F " Coy.
C.Q.M.S. Dyke	" C " Coy.		Sgt. J. V. Pope	" D " Coy.
C.S.M. S. Edridge	" F " Coy.		Sgt. R. Pritchard	" C " Coy.
Sgy. C. Field	" D " Coy.		Sgt. A. H. Ross	" F " Coy.
C.Q.M.S. W. E. Gilbert	" E " Coy.		Sgt. S. J. Stafford	" A " Coy.
Pte. F. Gray	" C " Coy.		Sgt. T. W. B. Ward	" D " Coy.
Sgt. J. Gregory	" H " Coy.		Sgt. A. Watts	" C " Coy.
Sgt. E. Harris	" J " Coy.		C.S.M. W. J. Way	" H " Coy.
Corp. H. Hatt.	" H " Coy.		Sgt. A. O. Wrintmore	" A " Coy.

The last recorded strength of the Battalion before " Stand Down " was :

" A " Coy.	329		" G " Coy.	164
" B " Coy.	255		" H " Coy.	213
" C " Coy.	293		" J " Coy.	94
" D " Coy.	195		H.Q. Coy.	101
" E " Coy.	836			
" F " Coy.	302		*Total*	2,782

A list of officers in their companies is given below :

H.Q. Company
Lt.-Col. C. R. B. Carrington, D. S. O., O.B.E.
Maj. Hon. C. M. Hore-Ruthven, C.M.G., D.S.O.
Maj. C. Wade
Capt. E. C. Barnes
Maj. T. Briscoe (M.O.)
Capt. H. Wayte Smith
Lt. F. G. Hunt
Lt. C. F. Burdge
Lt. H. Wright

2/Lt. F. A. Wheeler, M.M.
2/Lt. T. A. Deykes
2/Lt. W. E. George
2/Lt. J. A. Winter
2/Lt. E. P. Awdry, M.C., T.D.

" A " Company
Maj. Hon. R. A. Addington
Capt. J. Benson
Lt. J. R. Maundrell
Lt. L. Perrett
Lt. Rev. B. C. D. Palmer

"A" Company Continued:
Lt. H. R. Channings
Lt. J. Fulluck
Lt. R. Devening
Lt. H. Ayres
2/Lt. F. Freegard
2/Lt. F. Gardiner
2/Lt. E. Davis
2/Lt. Holman
2/Lt. O. Freegard

"B" Company
Maj. M. E. Cook, M.C.
Capt. C. H. Balch
Capt. A. K. James (M.O.)
Lt. A. S. Mittell, M.M.
Lt. F. W. Smith
Lt. A. G. L. Good
Lt. A. B. Granger
Lt. C. G. Higgins
Lt. G. C. Barnett
2/Lt. S. A. Marsh

"C" Company
Maj. W. V. D. Skrine, M.C.
Capt. I. A. Currey
Capt. A. R. Wheeler (M.O.)
Lt. M. A. Jackson
Lt. R. P. H. Hopkins
Lt. R. A. H. Stainer
Lt. E. W. Gale
Lt. A. R. Gough
2/Lt. H. J. Tucker

"D" Company
Maj. J. Morley
Capt. G. R. C. Soutar
Capt. J. G. S. Thomas, M.C. (M.O.)
Lt. W. Thompson
Lt. H. G. Russell
Lt. McEwen
Lt. J. Browning
Lt. J. E. Cope
Lt. W. J. Philpott

Lt. C. H. Fildes
Lt. W. Cameron Mackintosh

"E" Company
Maj. C. S. Williams, M.C.
Capt. F. Berryman
Capt. J. Shipway, D.C.M.
Capt. C. R. Lewis
Capt. L. H. Shrago (M.O.)
Capt. A. L. Williams
Capt. N. G. Cadman
Capt. C. M. Townsend
Capt. G. B. Jamieson
Lt. A. W. Hill (seconded)
Lt. H. S. Dickinson
Lt. H. Noble
Lt. J. W. T. Hauser
Lt. A. G. Drayson
Lt. W. J. Sheard
Lt. C. U. Parson, M.M.
Lt. L. H. B. Tufft
Lt. C. A. Rowley
Lt. F. Jordon
Lt. G. Goward
Lt. S. Waite
Lt. P. V. F. Gray, M.M.
Lt. W. H. Graham
Lt. W. J. Jackson
Lt. W. Davey
Lt. P. W. Edwards
2/Lt. G. G. Hathaway
2/Lt. J. W. G. Kershaw
2/Lt. H. J. Reckless
2/Lt. A. V. G. Hichisson
2/Lt. T. S. E. Palmer
2/Lt. F. J. Wade
2/Lt. R. G. Ferris
2/Lt. G. S. Harris
2/Lt. J. R. Laidlaw
2/Lt. H. Church
2/Lt. E. W. Church
2/Lt. A. J. Dyke
2/Lt. H. A. Strange
2/Lt. S. Silcox

"E" Company Continued:

2/Lt. J. Bushnell
2/Lt. F. V. R. Petley
2/Lt. R. H. Dunster
2/Lt. H. Griffin

"F" Company

Maj. R. H. Allan
Capt. P. J. H. Gunton
Capt. W. H. Royal (M.O.)
Lt. E. G. Harding
Lt. S. G. Blythe
Lt. J. R. Hannam
Lt. A. E. Grant
Lt. W. G. Pearce
Lt. R. Travers
Lt. H. W. Brown
Lt. W. Clark
Lt. R. G. Maurice
Lt. M. G. Slade
Lt. T. P. Morris
2/Lt. T. W. Wildin
2/Lt. A. G. Brackenbury

"G" Company

Maj. A. A. Soames
Capt. H. I. Fairclough
Capt. E. B. Hickson (M.O.)
Lt. R. Reeves
Lt. H. Adams
Lt. R. Jones
2/Lt. G. Tordoff
2/Lt. Donithorne-Clark
2/Lt. J. Short

"H" Company

Maj. M. S. D. Day, M.C.
Capt. H. Gold
Capt. W. G. Ayres (M.O.)
Lt. D. A. C. Hillier
Lt. R. V. Pegler
Lt. F. E. Birthill
Lt. M. Hughes
Lt. L. C. Woodcock
2/Lt. W. H. Gardener

"J" Company

Maj. A. Lambert
Lt. S. Chambers
Lt. P. Rogers
2/Lt. W. A. Tolley

"Fear God, honour the King."

2ND. BATTALION WILTSHIRE HOME GUARD
Appeal by Mr. Eden for Local Defence Volunteers

ON 14th May 1940, at 9 p.m., Mr. Eden made his broadcast appeal for volunteers to join the Local Defence Volunteers. Enrolment forms had already been received by the Police, and applicants were directed to report to them.

Formation of Local Defence Volunteers

ON 16th May 1940 Col. Hon. A F. Stanley, D.S.O. attended a meeting at Lockeridge House, Marlborough, which was arranged by Gen. Sir Francis Gathorne-Hardy. At this meeting Battalion areas were defined, and Col. Stanley was instructed to form a battalion in the area of Malmesbury, comprising the town of Malmesbury and its rural district.

Next day, 17th May, Col. Stanley discussed with Inspector Edwards of the Malmesbury Police the boundaries of proposed platoons, as they were then called and a map was drawn up showing the civil parish boundaries. The platoon areas arranged were Malmesbury (including Brokenborough, St. Paul Without and Lea), Crudwell (including Oaksey and Charlton), Sherston (including Luckington, Alderton, Sopworth and Easton Grey), Hullavington (including Corston and Norton), Great Somerford (including Little Somerford, Brinkworth and Dauntsey) and Minety (including Somerford Common).

Platoon commanders were selected by Col. Stanley, and a meeting was held at the Town Hall at 10.30 a.m. on 24th May 1940. Commanders were appointed as follows :

Malmesbury	Col. Rex Osborne, D.S.O., M.C.
Crudwell	Mr. Hugh Baker
Sherston	Capt. E. Greene, M.C.
Hullavington	Maj. Noel Wilson
Gt. Somerford	Col. W. L. Palmer, M.C.
Minety	Capt. G. Raimes

On 24th May 1940, eighty ·303 rifles and ammunition, and some denim overalls were delivered to the Police, and these were issued next day to platoon leaders. That night armed patrols were organised in all villages to look out for paratroops and suspicious looking individuals, and to guard vulnerable points and likely landing places. Rifles were issued to ex-servicemen with previous experience of a rifle, but no ammunition was issued for the first night or two, until those who carried rifles had got more used to carrying them.

On the 25th May platoon commanders held meetings and went round villages to enrol more recruits.

At the meeting in Malmesbury, Dr. Hodge (Mayor of Malmesbury) took the chair, and Col. Rex Osborne addressed the meeting and asked for recruits. The meeting was described as a " flop " and another " parashot " meeting was arranged for 27th May at 6 p.m.

The headquarters of the Local Defence Volunteers were established at the Police Station, and all letters, reports and messages were sent there or to Col. Stanley at Sopworth.

Later, headquarters was moved to a room at the Town Hall, which was lent rent free by the Malmesbury Borough Council.

At the end of June 1940, Maj. E. van Cutsem, M.C., took over the duties of adjutant, and assisted Col. Stanley. A telephone was installed in the office on 26th Aug.

About this time a few alterations were made in command and organisation of platoons, owing to the departure of Col. Rex Osborne and Capt. Raimes for duty with the Regular Army. Capt. C. C. Craig took over Malmesbury, and Minety Platoon was added to Crudwell. A separate platoon was formed at Luckington, under Capt. Hartman.

In December 1940 Col. Palmer took over the temporary command of the Battalion while Col. Stanley was away. His company area was taken over by Maj. D. Marsh. Col. Stanley returned in March 1941.

Title of Battalion. When first organised, the Battalion was called Malmesbury Local Defence Volunteer Battalion. Subsequently, at Mr. Churchill's suggestion, the Local Defence Volunteers came to be called the " Home Guard ", and the Battalion was called the Malmesbury Area Battalion Home Guard. Finally it became the 2nd Battalion Wiltshire Home Guard, and received the privilege of wearing the badge of the Wiltshire Regiment.

Commanders. When first organised, platoon and section commanders had no rank and were called platoon and section leaders. The men were called volunteers. The original platoon areas were reorganised as company areas, and village detachments became platoons or sections. Commanders of companies and platoons wore a piece of black braid on their shoulder straps, and N.C.O.s were given ordinary chevrons.

This continued until February 1941, when it was decided that company and platoon leaders should be given commissions as Home Guard officers. The change was received with little approval and even misgiving. The first lists of appointments appeared in Southern Command Orders to take effect from 1st Feb. 1941, and included the following :

Hon. A. F. Stanley, D.S.O., Col. (retired)	to be Lt.-Col.
Charles Curtis Craig	,, ,, Maj.
Edward Greene, M.C., Capt. (retired)	,, ,, Maj.
Charles William Sholto Douglas	,, ,, Maj.
Noel Stanley Wilson, Maj. (retired)	,, ,, Maj.
Edward C. L. van Cutsem, M.C., Capt. (retired)	,, ,, Maj.
Duncan Marsh	,, ,, Maj.
Hugh Baker	,, ,, Maj.
William Llewellen Palmer, M.C., Bt.-Col. (retired)	,, ,, Maj.
Walter Edward Snelling	,, ,, Lt.

and other appointments as captains and lieutenants.

48

At the end of March 1942, Lt.-Col. H. H. Stoney, D.S.O., who was in command of Crudwell Platoon, took over command of the Battalion on Col. Stanley's retirement on reaching the age limit for Home Guard officers. At the same time Maj. Craig and Maj. H. Baker were similarly retired.

Defences

One of the first tasks of company commanders was to reconnoitre their areas and note vulnerable points, such as railway bridges, likely enemy landing grounds, and observation points, and to take action to patrol them. O.P's were manned at night.

Several authorities, including the Wiltshire County Council, erected road-blocks, and lines of defence, and anti-tank ditches were constructed. The village defences were not fitted in with them, and conferences with Regular Army officers were held to co-ordinate the defences. The rôle of villages was not defined. In the early days the Local Defence Volunteers had expected to die in the last ditch, but their real rôle was to report to regular striking forces, and to harass and delay the enemy until that force arrived.

Some platoons thought that, as Home Guards, it was their duty to defend their village. Some villages were called " centres of resistance ". The strength and training and weapons of village platoons, however, did not permit them to do this effectively, and it was decided that all platoons should be mobile. They were to think less of defending their villages and more of harassing the enemy by any possible means. Company and platoon defence schemes were drawn up to make this clear.

At the same time, War Office instructions said Home Guards were not guerillas. They were not to sacrifice their lives needlessly, but they must harass the enemy by taking advantage of their intimate knowledge of their own fields and the areas near their villages.

The town of Malmesbury became an anti-tank island ; that is, the use of the roads through Malmesbury was to be denied to the enemy.

The strength of the company in Malmesbury was not great enough to hold the perimeter of the town, and after tests by practical exercises, it was decided to hold three posts in Malmesbury ; at the railway station, Steeple, and Holloway. Approaches to the posts were covered by spigot mortar fire.

The entrance to the town at the Silk Mills and the narrow roads near the Triangle were covered by fighting patrols from the Steeple Post.

One platoon was in reserve for counter attack and to look out for infiltration between posts.

Action Against Attack by Paratroops

In 1943, as risk of sea invasion receded, it was decided that there should be no defended localities, and that the only vulnerable point in Malmesbury was the

E.K.C.O. factory at Cowbridge. The Malmesbury Company was therefore used to supplement the defences of the factory.

During this year wireless sets were received and one of the Malmesbury platoons was converted into a signalling section. It was hoped with these sets to keep in touch with platoons who were operating against paratroops. Exercises were held to try this out and to test the best means of helping in the defence of the airfields at Hullavington and Kemble.

In 1943, " G " Company at E.C.K.O. factory was converted into " A " L.A.A. Troop, and the dual rôle of manning the A.A. guns and ground defence of the works, supported by " A " Company (Malmesbury), who were to hold positions on outskirts near Cowbridge Lodge.

In an exercise held to test the defences, the works were overrun in twenty minutes after zero hour. As a result of this, it was decided to allot " A " Company to the outer defence of the factory as their position on action stations, leaving Malmesbury undefended.

American Units

Various American units were stationed at Charlton Park. It was arranged with them that they would deal with any parachutists who fell near their camp. Their presence here gave the Home Guard a chance to compare their dress for fighting order with that of the Germans. Some Home Guards had been confused by the similarity of the American and German steel helmets and equipment.

Administration

Maj. van Cutsem was appointed adjutant at the end of June 1940, and he obtained the services of Miss Davis as typist, clerk and general secretary on 12th July 1940. Sgt. C. A. Hughes was employed one day a week as storeman and clerk to issue clothing and stores, and in November 1941 he was engaged on a full time basis.

An imprest account for expenses was opened in October 1941.

In the early days rifles and clothing were issued without receipts or vouchers, and records had to be made up from notes in a note-book. The ledgers were not made correct until a regular A. & Q. officer, Capt. C. F. Royston, R.A. was appointed in June 1942.

A regular adjutant, Capt. C. R. Pennick of the Middlesex Regiment (attached 30th Wiltshires) was appointed in February 1942.

Mr. C. E. Meakin of Minety, Chairman of the Malmesbury Rural District Council, was enlisted as Permanent Staff Instructor on 15th May 1941.

Battalion Headquarters was moved from the Town Hall to Abbey House in May 1942, and signal communications were improved.

The use of pigeons for message carrying was arranged, and the loft of Mr. Bishop of Gastons was utilised. Maj. Duke Moore organised this.

Inspections and Parades

On 6th Oct. 1940 the Battalion paraded for a service at the Abbey, which was attended by H.M. Queen Mary. It was a wet inclement day. Platoons marched past Her Majesty, and the following letter was received by Col. Stanley from her equerry :

" I am commanded by Queen Mary to tell you how delighted she was last Sunday to have the opportunity of seeing the members of the Home Guard at Malmesbury, and to say that Her Majesty was much impressed by their smartness on parade. Everything went off splendidly, in spite of the weather."

The next Battalion parade was for the opening of " War Weapons " Week in 1941, in conjunction with the Civil Defence Services and Regular Army representatives. The parade assembled at the railway station and the procession was formed up there. The parade marched past Queen Mary, who was on a dais in the Cross Hayes, and then formed up in the Square for the speeches at the opening ceremony.

Similar parades were held for " Warships " Week in 1942, " Wings for Victory " Week in 1943 and " Salute the Soldier " Week in 1944. The improvement in the drill and turnout on each occasion was remarkable.

Training

In the early days the training of platoons depended on local instructors. Later outside assistance was made available. For some months, beginning February 1941, Capt. Dodgson and an N.C.O. from the striking force were detailed to come from Tidworth and give lectures to platoons in turn. At the same time, N.C.O.s were sent for training as instructors at week-end courses arranged for Home Guards. Home Guard schools were opened for training of N.C.O.s, platoon, company and battalion commanders.

After the regular adjutant was appointed, battalion classes for junior officers and N.C.O.s were held on Monday evenings. Instruction included giving words of command, fire orders, firing point instruction, and, later, battle drill. This led to a great improvement as both officers and N.C.O.s gained confidence.

T.E.W.T.s were held on Sunday mornings for a limited number of N.C.O.s from every company.

Later, the Travelling Wing from the Home Guard school at Denbies visited the battalion and gave instruction. Tactical exercises without troops were held, to work out the best method of dealing with paratroops.

As the training of platoons progressed, they were taught to work together as a company.

Latterly ammunition was available for rifle shooting, and the standard improved. Home Guard rifle course was laid down, but it was never fired owing to range difficulties.

Battle innoculation practices were not carried out because no suitable ground was available.

In " B ", " E " and " G " Companies men were trained for proficiency tests, and a good proportion passed and were awarded, and were very proud of their badge.

In other companies officers or men were unwilling to submit to the test. This was a disadvantage to those companies, as they had no real test of the standard of their training.

In some companies, particularly in " B " Company (Snelling) the value of training officers and N.C.O.s was realised early.

Comferences of platoon commanders were held weekly, and this led later to weekly conferences and discussions with N.C.O.s. At these conferences ideas were worked out and all difficulties were discussed. They went through battle drill and the issue of orders and the best system of passing messages quickly. These ideas were then worked out in a tactical exercise with troops, and the mistakes were thrashed out afterwards. The progress made was remarkable, and this in turn led to the co-operation of platoons as a company. Training films were used to good advantage, and they gave us ideas which could be applied to our training. The films also showed us how to recognise enemy tanks and armoured vehicles, and the differences between our own and the German.

" D " Day

About a month before " D " Day it was thought that the Germans might counter our preparations by landing parachutists and damaging important points on railways. All bridges and other vulnerable points on main lines were guarded at night.

It entailed a night on duty after a hard day's work, but all men took their turn. They felt that this might give them their chance of seeing something, and they enjoyed it.

It was very practical training. Magazines were charged and guards or patrols, with their reliefs, were arranged. Places were fixed up where reliefs could sleep, and a hot meal was provided.

Feeding Exercise

The feeding of the Home Guard platoons, when engaged in operations against an enemy, presented many problems. In the early days it was thought that the men could obtain their food by going back to their homes for their meals. In active operations it was realised that this dispersion was not feasible for many obvious reasons. It was therefore arranged that when the Home Guardsman reported on standing-to, he should bring with him his rations for twenty-four hours. In addition, arrangements were made to send out sufficient stocks of food to a selected grocer in the village to provide Home Guard requirements for two weeks. In each platoon a feeding centre was authorised to comply with Ministry of Food regulations.

Cooking was to be done by W.V.S. or Home Guard wives, as arranged by the platoon. There were not sufficient cooking utensils, and these had to be supplemented from private sources.

Satisfactory plans were made, and on a selected day a feeding exercise was held to test them.

Captain Royston had conferences with company second-in-commands and platoon Q.M.S's to explain and discuss the arrangements. The rations were put ready on a platoon basis and sent out to all platoon headquarters with a suggested diet sheet for the meals. The exercise was timed to last from seven p.m. on a Saturday to one p.m. on the Sunday, i.e., including supper, breakfast and dinner. It was held on 15–16 August, 1942.

During the period training was carried out, but the actual programme was left to the discretion of company commanders.

Miscellaneous Notes

On 20th Nov. 1940 at about 18.20 hours Volunteer J. J. Langley of Charlton Platoon saw a plane come down in a field at Dolman's Farm, Hankerton. He hid in a hedge and as the crew advanced he called out " Halt—nationality please," and received the answer : " Don't shoot, we are Poles." He took the men to the farm and sent for his platoon commander, Rev. F. Hudson, who telephoned to Kemble Aerodrome. He was asked to guard the plane, and mounted a guard in two-hour shifts until 08.00 hours the next day.

This action was commended by Brig. Studd, Commander of Salisbury Plain Area, who wrote that he considered Volunteer Langley had acted in an exemplary manner, and gave instructions that a note of the event should be attached to his documents. He also thought that the platoon commander had acted with most commendable promptitude and efficiency.

Petrol Supplies and Earmarking of Cars

Platoon commanders were responsible for seeing that petrol pumps were dismantled nightly, and in case of emergency, for the immobilisation of all petrol.

A certain number of cars in each platoon were earmarked for use in case of invasion. When the scheme was first started a liberal number of cars was allowed, but this was gradually cut down. It was barely sufficient.

Bicycles

Most platoons used their bicycles to move quickly from one end of their area to another. Other platoons were less mobile-minded and wanted buses. There was an allowance for a limited number of bicycles, but the arrangement was never satisfactory.

Memories of a Platoon Commander

I was given command of a platoon early in 1940. It had done some elementary training in its weapons, but was not organised and had no discipline, except that born of Home Guard willingness. Home Guard discipline was a strange thing. It was the discipline of good will—those who had no good will had no discipline except the force of public opinion, and no one knew what to do if a man should refuse to obey an order. Later we found out about all that.

The first step was to organise the platoon in three sections. A commander and second in command were selected for each section, and sections were made up from men in the same part of the village. This facilitated warning for parade and calling out in emergency.

Section commanders were made to inspect their sections and the rifles under the eye of the platoon commander. They were very diffident and terrified of giving a word of command. Doing this gave them confidence and a sense of responsibility.

Drill was taught by falling in, and on the march to the place where training was to be carried out. Strict attention was paid to dressing and covering off on the march. The second in command marched in the rear. " Eyes right " and " left " was practised on the march until it was perfect.

Discipline began to grow.

On the drill night during the week in summer, training was given in some item of individual training. This was practised on the following Sunday under section commanders or in a platoon exercise. There was a conference after every exercise.

In the winter advantage was taken of all fine evenings to do outdoor night training.

At the end of a period of individual training, sections were practised in working together, and platoon exercises to round up parachutists at night or to locate tanks in woods were carried out. Great attention was paid to issue of orders and every man knowing his job. The platoon had done weapon training, but had little or no practice, and had never fired its ·300 rifle.

Tests of elementary training were carried out, and after a short period the platoon was taken on the range. We started by grouping at 25 yards. Any men who failed were tested and section commanders were taught to find and correct their fault. We then went back to 100 and 200 yards. Ammunition was sufficient to fire only five rounds per man.

Records were kept, and each Sunday the results of the day's shooting were worked out, and the men told which section had the best average.

At the end of this training each man fired five rounds with his own ·300 rifle with surprisingly good results—one possible and several good scores.

The Lewis Gun team was exercised in the same way, starting by single shot grouping at 25 yards, and then going back to 200 yards.

All aspects of our job as a Home Guard platoon were tried out on exercises. Rounding up parachutists : searching for parachutists who had gone to ground ; ambushes for tanks ; ambushes against invasion troops, and then scattering and reassembling ; best use of Northover ; delaying actions ; observing an area and reporting quickly, and moving quickly on bicycles ; searching a wood.

We learnt our shortcomings and used our imagination to visualise every possible enemy action.

We did not learn to defend the village, because there were not enough men to do it.

We practised working with R.A.F. in defence of an aerodrome and acted as enemy in attacking it, and showed them the weakness of their defence.

The Battalion parades at Savings Weeks were a great help in making the men proud of themselves. A few men never toed the line, but most of them were wonderful and keen.

We worked out a system of calling out men quickly at night and practised it. The call-out was timed for about 3 a.m., so that the men could go straight to their milking. As they arrived, or at the end of the exercise, they were given a cup of tea. During several months we had a night watch to look out for parachutists or incendiaries. The watch consisted of a commander and two men. The commander had one night duty every week, and the men had a turn once a fortnight.

Command

The command and administration of a Home Guard battalion has been a difficult job, but the enthusiasm of the volunteers simplified it. The conscripts introduced a bad spirit, and their heart in most cases was not in their service.

Without an efficient regular A. & Q. officer for administration, it would have been impossible. He kept in touch with company and platoon " Q " representatives, and taught them how to keep their records correctly.

At one time there was some friction between the Regular Army permanent staff and the Home Guard officers and N.C.O.s, partly because the former were paid. When the Home Guard realised how much help they received from them, they gave them their confidence.

It is very necessary to have efficient regular officers, and not just those who are too old for more active employment.

Honours and Awards

Com.-in-Chf.'s Certificates were awarded to the under-mentioned officers and N.C.O.s :

Name	Unit	Date
Sgt. E. P. Edwards	Brinkworth Platoon	Jan. 1942
Sgt. F. W. Horsham	Luckington Platoon	Jan. 1942
Sgt. R. A. Brookman	Hullavington Platoon	24 June 1942
Sgt. H. C. Starey	Crudwell Platoon	24 June 1942
Sgt. D. G. Brown	Seagry Platoon	20 Jan. 1943
C.S.M. G. N. Shelley	Malmesbury Company	20 Jan. 1943
Lt. H. V. Bonner	Malmesbury Company	9 June 1943

Name	Unit	Date
Sgt. W. Legg	Oaksey Platoon	9 June 1943
Sgt. W. J. Vining	Sherston Platoon	9 June 1943
Sgt. A. Hislop	Charlton Platoon	12 Jan. 1944
Sgt. A. Ward	Luckington Platoon	12 Jan. 1944
Lt. F. V. Knapp	Sherston Platoon	21 June 1944
Sgt. P. Lewis	Seagry Platoon	21 June 1944
Sgt. C. E. Timbrell	Minety Platoon	12 Jan. 1945
Sgt. A. E. Selby	Crudwell Platoon	12 Jan. 1945
Sgt. G. Quick	Brinkworth Platoon	12 Jan. 1945
Lt. W. R. Fry	Norton Platoon	12 Jan. 1945

O.B.E.

Lt.-Col. H. H. Stoney, D.S.O.		19 June 1943

B.E.M.

Sgt. R. M. Saunders, M.M.	Corston Platoon	12 Dec. 1944

Organisation and Strength on Stand down

Unit	Name of Officer	Appointment	Strength
H.Q. Coy.	Lt.-Col. H. H. Stoney, D.S.O., O.B.E.	Battalion Commander	70
	Maj. N. D. Hart	2 i/c Battalion	
	Capt. R. O. W. Arkwright	Adjutant	
	Capt. C. F. Royston	Capt. A. & Q.	
	Maj. B. L. Hodge	Medical Officer	
	Capt. R. H. Osborne, D.S.O., M.C.	Chief Guide and Liaison Officer	
	2/Lt. F. H. Wardle-Smith	2 i/c Guides	
	Lt. S. H. Pettifer	Gas and M.T Officer	
	Lt. P. J. Dickinson	Ammunition Officer	
	Lt. L. Gardiner	Junior Liaison Officer	
	Lt. Hon. C. Douglas	Officer i/c Snipers	
	Lt. S. G. Davey	Seconded A.C.F.	
	Lt. F. W. Henwood		
(Signal Pln.)	Lt. M. C. Ingram	Signals Officer	(27)
	2/Lt. C. W. Essex	Assistant Signal Officer	
(Intel. Pln.)	Lt. N. W. Evans	Intelligence Officer	(14)
" A " Coy.	Maj. H. V. Bonner	Company Commander	150
	Capt. G. N. Shelley	2 i/c Company	
	2/Lt. R. Butt	Company Ammunition Officer	
	Lt. C. G. Campbell, 2!Lt. J. H. F. Hulse, 2/Lt. A. Box, Lt. G. G. Newman, 2/Lt. A. May }	Platoon Commanders	

Unit	Name of Officer	Appointment	Strength
" B " Coy.	Maj. W. E. Snelling	Company Commander	211
	Capt. C. H. Shores	2 i/c Company	
	Lt. G. H. B. Chance	Company Intelligence Officer	
	2/Lt. A. B. Blanch	Assistant Intelligence Officer	
	Lt. Charles Jones, Lt. H. C. Starey, Lt. F. W. Constable, Lt. G. C. Todd	} Platoon Commanders	
" C " Coy.	Maj. E. Greene, M.C.	Company Commander	138
	Lt. F. V. Knapp, 2/Lt. W. Thompson, 2/Lt. W. J. Vining, Lt. F. W. Horsham, 2/Lt. R. Padfield, Lt. A. G. Jolliffe, 2/Lt. W. G. S. Parsons	} Platoon Commanders	
" D " Coy.	Maj. N. S. Wilson	Company Commander	110
	Lt. G. W. Sisum, Lt. R. A. Brookman, Lt. W. R. Fry	} Platoon Commanders	
" E " Coy.	Major E. P. Edwards	Company Commander	138
	Lt. C. G. Gully, Lt. F. Whitehead Lt. B. R. Pearce, Lt. C. Gawthropp, 2/Lt. E. P. Awdry	} Platoon Commanders	
" F " Coy.	Maj. W. L. Palmer, M.C.	Company Commander	72
	Capt. A. S. Martin, M.M.	2 i/c Company	
	Lt. F. S. Brind, M.M., Lt. D. G. Brown	} Platoon Commanders	
" G " Coy. (E.K.C.O.) (" A " L.A.A. Trp.)	Maj. E. A. Hider	Company Commander	82
	Capt. H. L. Cooley	2 i/c Company	
	Lt. N. R. W. Tanner, Lt. A. U. Emery	} Platoon Commanders	
" H " Coy. (Hullavington Aerodrome)	Maj. V. Whitaker	Company Commander	273
	Capt. F. Browdie	2 i/c Company	
	Lt. D. J. Dunne	Company Admin. Officer	
	Lt. Sleightholme, Lt. A. J. Long, Lt. W. Worrell, 2/Lt. L. H. Clifford, 2/Lt. R. Humble, 2/Lt. Merrick, 2/Lt. A. Hurst, 2/Lt. F. C. Warren, 2/Lt. D. H. Thorburn	} Platoon Commanders	

Battalion strength on Stand down : **1,244**

Retired Officers

Name	Appointment	Date of Commission		Date of Retirement	
Lt.-Col. Hon. A. F. Stanley, D.S.O.	Battalion Commander	1 Feb.	1942	1 March	1942
Maj. Hugh Baker	Commander " B " Coy.	1 Feb.	1941	1 July	1942
Maj. R. T. Chamen	Commander " A " Coy. 2 i/c Battalion	1 Feb.	1941	31 Dec.	1943
Capt. Viscount Coke	2 i/c " C " Coy.	1 Feb.	1941	(Posted 4th Norfolk Bn.) 9 April	1942
2/Lt. E. J. Couzens	Platoon Commander	1 Feb.	1941	5 Feb.	1942
Maj. C. C. Craig	Commander " A " Coy. and 2 i/c Battalion	1 Feb.	1941	31 March	1942
Maj. S. F. Deacon	Commander " H " Coy.	1 Dec.	1941	8 Feb.	1943
2/Lt. J. A. Else	Platoon Officer	1 May	1943	(Posted 6th Norfolk Bn.) 19 Aug.	1944
Capt. S. Gibson	2 i/c " H " Coy.	1 Dec.	1941	9 March	1943
Maj. J. Hirst	Commander " A " Coy.	1 Feb.	1941	12 July	1944
Capt. J. J. R. Hood	2 i/c " H " Coy.	1 Dec.	1941	11 Nov.	1943
Lt. F. James	Assistant Guide Officer	1 April	1942	1 Feb.	1944
Maj. D. Marsh	Commander " E " Coy.	1 Feb.	1941	31 March	1943
Capt. E. Duke Moore, D.S.O., T.D.		1 Aug.	1941	31 March	1942
Maj. R. M. Moore	Battalion Medical Officer	1 Feb.	1941	4 Dec.	1942
Lt. W. W. Pitter	Platoon Commander	1 Feb.	1942	17 May	1944
2/Lt. E. N. Ratcliffe	Platoon Officer	15 March	1943	17 July	1944
Capt. R. Tindle	Platoon Commander	1 Feb.	1941	21 Feb.	1942
Maj. E. van Cutsem, M.C.	Adjutant and 2 i/c Battalion	1 Feb.	1941	10 Dec.	1942

Stand down Parade, 3rd December 1944

The " stand down " parade of the 2nd Battalion on Sunday morning, 3rd Dec. 1944, took the form of an impressive drumhead service in the Cross Hayes, Malmesbury, the keynote of which was thankfulness and hope—thankfulness that its members had been privileged to be of service to the country in her hour of need, and hope that they might still be of service to their fellow men.

A large muster assembled for inspection by Maj.-Gen. R. N. Gale, D.S.O., O.B.E., M.C., the seven companies present being under the command of Lt.-Col. H. H. Stoney, D.S.O., Battalion Commander.

The parade was drawn up facing a dais on which were accommodated the following, who had helped the Home Guard in the past and who attended at the invitation of the Battalion Commander : Col. Hon. A. F. Stanley, D.S.O. (the original Battalion Commander), Maj. E. van Cutsem, M.C., Maj. D. Marsh, Maj. R. T. Chamen, Maj. E. Duke Moore (former senior officers), Maj. A. Heath (Senior Military Officer at Malmesbury), the Mayor and Mayoress of Malmesbury (Mr. and Mrs. Grabham), Mr. C. Meakin (Chairman, Rural District Council) and Mrs. Meakin, Mrs. Wyborn (representing W.V.S.) and Miss Davis (Chief Clerk at Battalion Headquarters, representing Women Home Guard Auxiliaries).

A band of the Royal Air Force stood in the rear of the parade.

Upon the arrival of the inspecting general, the " General Salute " was given, and General Gale, who commands the 6th Airborne Division which gained such fame in the landing in Normandy, proceeded to inspect the Battalion, chatting with several of the men, some of them old soldiers who served with him in the last war.

The service was conducted by the Battalion Padre, the Rev. F. Hudson, vicar of Charlton. It opened with the hymn " Now thank we all our God ", following which Col. Stoney read the lesson from Ecclesiasticus xliv. 1-15 (" Let us now praise famous men "), and the hymn " Fight the good fight " was sung. Prayers then offered by the Padre included that first used by Sir Francis Drake when he sailed into Cadiz to " singe the King of Spain's beard " (" O Lord God, when Thou givest to Thy servants to endeavour on any great matter "), and these were followed by the hymn " Onward Christian Soldiers ".

Addressing the parade, Gen. Gale said : " I regard it as a great honour and a great privilege to have been asked to come and see you to-day on this very important occasion. It is my privilege as a young general, to command a division of troops who have to fight, and have fought, the Hun in this war. As a youngster, I fought in the last war. It was with terrific pride that I walked round with your commanding officer to-day and looked into the faces of men who are the fathers of the young chaps I have the honour of commanding. It is blatantly obvious, when one has the privilege to do that, why the young man of to-day is the magnificent chap he is.

" As far as the Home Guard itself is concerned, there can be no question of the enormous service that it has contributed in the past four years. I, as a responsible officer commanding, know how much, from the point of view of defence of this country, earlier on, we depended upon you. My position is, perhaps, a little peculiar, because, as the commander of an airborne division, I know what cognisance in my plans I have had to have of the equivalent but not so good a force on the Continent. One word as to the future : This business has got to go on. I am not the Government, and I have no power, but so far as I, as an individual, have any say in the matter, it must go on. We have had this ghastly war, and we are going to try and stop another one, but if another one comes, it will come very suddenly. We have seen many of these V1's and V2's, and we know the immense power of airborne forces, therefore this country will want its Home Guard in the future. Let us pray it will not need it, but certainly it must have it ready.

" In command of my men, I am acutely conscious of the fact that every man is in two halves—the man whom I command and the woman or the family that he leaves at home. When a man loses his life in battle, this duality is brought home to one very acutely. All the time that you have been giving your leisure hours to work and to training, which may have been pleasant from your point of view, has meant a sacrifice in the home ; therefore, while wishing all of you present every happiness for the future, and whilst thanking you personally for what you have done, I should like to say that those remarks are equally true, and come equally from the heart to the women in the homes, who have put up with all they have had to put up with for the last four years."

Voicing the thanks of the Battalion to Gen. Gale, Col. Stoney said that his airborne division won great fame in Normandy, and but for the skill, fighting spirit, tenacity and endurance of that division, it might never have been possible to exploit the success of our landings in Normandy. The Colonel also thanked the Mayor for arranging the details of the parade, and for his work and help as Chairman of the Borough Invasion Committee.

"I want to congratulate you on a duty well done," said the Commanding Officer, " particularly the old Local Defence Volunteers, who showed us the way, the platoon and section commanders, the specialists who trained us, and all our permanent staff. But above all I should like to single out the platoon commander, who really was the backbone of the Home Guard ; he bore the burden, set the example, and displayed the enthusiasm. Remember that we are still Home Guard ; we are not disbanded, and until we are disbanded we have got to keep our organisation in being. You have set a wonderful example to the country ; now, let us hand it on to the cadets. I want to say ' Good-bye ' to you all, and to thank you for the help and loyalty which you have given to me personally and to your company commanders, without which we could have done nothing."

The National Anthem was played by the band, which afterwards headed a march of the Battalion through the main streets of the town, in the course of which the salute was taken by Gen. Gale outside the King's Arms Hotel, while the R.A.F. band, which had accompanied the singing of the hymns during the service, played the Regimental March of the Wiltshire Regiment, " The 'Vly be on the Turmuts ".

Three notable absentees from the parade were Privates D. G. Kemp (Crudwell), S. Milne (Sopworth), and F. Scott (Little Somerford), who were selected to represent the Battalion at the ceremonial stand down Parade of the Home Guard in London.

3rd BATTALION WILTSHIRE HOME GUARD

16 *May* 1940

The Warminster Battalion of the Local Defence Volunteers was inaugurated. The area covered by the Battalion was approximately the Warminster Police District with the exception of a few villages, and this has remained unaltered.

Col. Sir George Herbert, Bart., T.D., took command with his headquarters at Knoyle House, East Knoyle, and Maj. S. T. Grigg became his second in command.

The Battalion was split into companies as shown below.

" A " Company. Westbury and immediate district, commanded by Capt. G. G. Hoare.

" B " Company. Warminister and Wylye Valley, stretching as far as Wylye in the west and including Sutton Veny, commanded by Lt.-Col. Budgeon, who retired early in the summer of 1940 and was succeeded by Brig.-Gen. E. Harding Newman, C.M.G., D.S.O.

" C " Company. Horningsham, Corsley, Maiden Bradley, The Deverills and district, commanded by Lt.-Col. A. E. Newland.

" D " Company. Mere, Zeals, Stourton, Kilmington and districts, commanded by Lt.-Col. E. S. Godman.

" E " Company. Chilmark, Tisbury, Hindon, East Knoyle and districts, commanded by Lt.-Col. C. T. Marshall Smith.

" F " Company. The Donheads, Swallowcliffe, Berwick St. John, Tollard Royal, Anstey, Charlton, Ludwell, Semley and districts, commanded by Lt.-Col. A. C. Allen.

All companies were more or less organised by 3 June 1940, and training commenced within a few days.

At the end of July, 1940, the Local Defence Volunteers were renamed " The Home Guard ". During the whole of this period the training consisted of Sundays and two evenings a week. The companies also formed guards at certain V.P.s and O.P.s and each village and town found patrols of one N.C.O. and six men during the hours of darkness.

The ceiling strength of the Battalion was fixed at 2,500 officers and men which was later altered to 2,400. The numbers never reached this figure, and after compulsory direction to the Home Guard was instituted early in 1942, fluctuated around 2,150.

In June 1944, " B " Company was split, Warminister including Sutton Veny and Bishopstrow remained " B " Company under the command of Brig.-Gen. E. Harding Newman. The Wylye Valley, down to Wylye and including Imber and Chittern, became " G " Company under the command of Maj. G. Channer, D.S.O.

21 *June* 1940

Lt.-Col. Godman relinquished his appointment of " D " Company Commander and was succeeded by Maj. H. C. Maydon.

1 *Feb.* 1941

All Home Guard officers appointments were regularised by Southern Command Order 471 of 1941. The Commanding Officer was appointed Lt.-Col., Second in Command and company commanders appointed majors, Company seconds in command captains, platoon commanders lieutenants and platoon officers second lieutenants.

A. S. Collett, Esq., was appointed major and took over command of " F " Company from Lt.-Col. A. C. Allen, who relinquished his appointment on rejoining the Regular Army.

24 *Feb.* 1941

Maj. G. M. Atkinson, D.S.O., was appointed major and Second in Command of the Battalion, and replaced Maj. Grigg who had been re-employed in the Regular Army and ordered overseas.

15 *July* 1941

The first permanent staff instructor, Sgt. E. H. Dunford, was posted to the Battalion from the Wiltshire Regiment Depot, Devizes.

27 *Oct.* 1941

As the result of regular and permanent adjutants being authorised for the Home Guard, Capt. H. F. N. Powell, of the Wiltshire Regiment, was posted to the 3rd Battalion.

5 *Nov.* 1941

Information was received that the Wiltshire Home Guard battalions had been numbered and that the Warminster Battalion would be known as the 3rd (Warminster) Battalion Wiltshire Home Guard.

15 *Nov.* 1941

Capt. A. R. Clare Smith was appointed major and took over command of " G " Company, vice Maj. G. Channer who resigned on grounds of ill health.

Capt. L. R. French was promoted major and took command of " B " Company as Brig.-Gen. Harding Newman had relinquished his appointment also on the grounds of health.

29 *Jan.* 1942

Col. Sir George Herbert, the Commanding Officer died suddenly at Bath, to the great grief of all who knew him.

31 *Jan.* 1942

Major G. M. Atkinson, Second in Command, was appointed Lt.-Col. and took over the command of the Battalion.

1 *Feb.* 1942

Brig.-Gen. R. F. A. Hobbs, C.B., C.M.G., D.S.O., was appointed major and Second in Command of the Battalion.

1 *March* 1942

Lt. C. R. Algar was appointed major and took command of " C " Company, vice Maj. A. E. Newland who retired.

1 *June* 1942

It was decided to form another company to be known as " H " Company consisting of the Stourton, Kilmington and Maiden Bradley districts. The two former villages to be taken from " D " Company and the latter from " C " Company.

Capt. G. F. Aldridge, of " D " Company, was appointed major and took command.

10 *July* 1942

The War Office having sanctioned regular captains for administrative and quartermasters' duties to relieve adjutants for concentration on training, Capt. L. G. Butcher, R.A., was appointed and posted to the 3rd Battalion as Captain A. & Q. duties.

1 *Aug.* 1942

Capt. W. G. B. White was appointed major and took over command of " D " Company, vice Maj. H. C. Maydon who retired owing to ill health.

15 *Feb.* 1943

Battalion Headquarters moved from Knoyle House, East Knoyle, to Melrose, 5 High Street, Warminister, on the recommendation of the South Wiltshire Sub-Area Commander.

15 *April* 1943

R.S.M. Hewitt, The Buffs, arrived to take over temporarily from Capt. L. G. Butcher pending the appointment of a new officer for A. & Q. duties.

17 *April* 1943

Capt. L. G. Butcher was transferred for duty at a prisoner of war camp and R.S.M. Hewitt took over.

16 *May* 1943

For the first time since the Battalion was formed all the companies came together and paraded at Warminister to celebrate the third anniversary of the Home Guard, and marched past Brig. Gregson Ellis, O.B.E., Grenadier Guards, who took the salute. They were headed by the pipe band of the Fife and Forfar Yeomanry who were stationed in the town at the time.

There were 1,750 officers, N.C.O.s and men on parade out of a battalion strength of 2,278.

24 *June* 1943

Capt. C. P. Arthur, the Wiltshire Regiment, was appointed Captain A. & Q. duties and took over from R.S.M. Hewitt.

16 *Dec.* 1943

A light A.A. troop was formed from some of the employees of the Great Western Railway in " A " Company at Westbury, to be known as the 28th (G.W.R.) L.A.A. Troop under the command of Lt. W. G. Cockell who was promoted to captain on 1st March 1944.

30 *Jan.* 1944

The Director General Home Guard, Maj.-Gen. The Viscount, Bridgeman, D.S.O., M.C., visited Warminster and was present during an exercise between " A " and " B " Companies.

6 *Sept.* 1944

The first instructions were received regarding the Standing down of the Home Guard.

3 *Dec.* 1944

In conjunction with the Stand down parades held throughout the British Isles, the 3rd Battalion paraded at Warminster and marched through the town accompanied by the bugles and drums of the 3rd Wiltshire Battalion Army Cadet Force. They then formed a hollow square at the Football Field and were addressed and inspected by the Lord Lieutenant of Wiltshire, Col. The Duke of Somerset, O.B.E., D.S.O. The Battalion then marched past him at his saluting base at the Regal Cinema, Weymouth Street, where they gave the final salute.

There were 1,107 officers and men on parade out of a total of 2,138.

Arms

In 1940 the average allotment of arms per company consisted of about half a dozen ordinary Short Lee Enfield rifles, and shot guns and pistols as procurable, augmented shortly after by pikes and bludgeons.

Month by month arms gradually arrived and were distributed to companies.

By the time the Home Guard were ordered to stand down the arms held by the Battalion were as follows :

Rifles, ·300, 1,042 ; Rifles, ·300 E.Y., 116 ; Browning Automatic Rifles, ·300, 10 ; Lewis Machine-guns, ·300, 38 ; Vickers M. Machine-guns, ·300, 4 ; Browning M. Machine-guns, ·300, 4 ; Vickers M. Machine-guns, ·303, 3 ; Browning M.M.G. Twin, ·303, 12 ; Sten Guns, 9 m.m., 455 ; Spigot Mortars, 29 ; Smith Guns, 3 ; 2-Pounder Anti-tank Guns, 6.

Ammunition

In the early days ammunition, both for operational and training purposes, was very short, but the situation very gradually grew easier and by the end of 1943 there was enough and to spare.

4TH BATTALION WILTSHIRE HOME GUARD

IT was in response to Mr. Eden's stirring appeal that Brig.-Gen. Lord Roundway, late Grenadier Guards, was entrusted with the task of organising the force for the Trowbridge and Devizes Division of the county.

Lord Roundway called a meeting of ex-officers at the Territorial Offices, Trowbridge, on Monday, 20th May at which were present :

Brig.-Gen. Lord Roundway (Chairman), Col. R. W. Awdry, Lt.-Col. Sir G. R. Blake, Mr. W. H. Ewart, Maj. E. A. Machay, Police Superintendent Meaney.

We were told that we should form the Trowbridge and Devizes Group Local Defence Volunteers covering an area of approximately 200 square miles of varied country comprising four industrial centres, Trowbridge, Devizes, Melksham and Bradford-on-Avon and a large area of Wiltshire Downs and Salisbury Plain. The area is approximately rectangular measuring in a straight line 21 miles by 11. There was no limit placed upon the numbers to be enrolled.

Our primary duty was to watch the countryside at night and, if necessary, to give the alarm. Lord Roundway asked if it would be possible to have a few men out that same night for observation. Some present thought it could be done, and it *was* done, the weapons produced being one or two revolvers and a few twelve bore shotguns.

The organisation of the area was to be based on five companies :

1. Trowbridge   under the command of Maj. E. A. Mackay
2. Bradford-on-Avon   ,,   ,,   ,,   ,, Capt. Whitehead
3. Melksham   ,,   ,,   ,,   ,, Lt.-Col. Sir G. R. Blake
4. Devizes   ,,   ,,   ,,   ,, Mr. W. H. Ewart
5. Market Lavington   ,,   ,,   ,,   ,, Col. R. W. Awdry

From the moment of Mr. Eden's appeal large numbers of men began to visit the police stations to have their names placed upon the roll, with the result that not only were observation posts being manned nightly all over the area but patrols were operating along the roads, whilst road-blocks were improvised from farm wagons, etc. and manned by parties of six men under a post leader, from dusk to dawn. Identity cards of all comers were examined at night and even the passengers in the omnibuses then running were checked, a proceeding not always appreciated by late travellers.

The rate of applications for enrolment is indicated by the following figures :

Actual Enrolments

28 May	1,200
11 June	2,010
18 June	2,100
2 July	2,609

During June a few ·303 rifles with a small amount of ammunition and " Molotoff Cocktails ", an improvised anti-tank weapon of an inflamable nature used successfully in Russia and invented by M. Molotoff, had been issued to the various companies and patrols. The " uniform " of the Local Defence Volunteers consisted up to now, of an armlet and field service cap, but a few denim suits were gradually being issued.

On the 2nd July Brig.-Gen. Lord Roundway, the Battalion Commander telephoned the first " stand by " order at 1.10 a.m., and throughout the Battalion area, volunteers were in readiness for " action stations " until well into the day.

In this month Brig. G. Darwell, M.C., recently invalided from the Regular Forces, took over the command of the Devizes Company with Mr. Ewart as Second in Command, and in the same month Col. R. W. Awdry resigned command of the Lavington Company, owing to pressure of county work, Maj. S. C. Welchman taking over from him.

In August, the Local Defence Volunteers received its permanent nomenclature, namely THE HOME GUARD, and the force began to take on a military appearance with the issue of battle dress, boots, gaiters and other items of equipment, together with a further issue of rifles.

During the following winter months, much hard work was put in on very intensive training in the different weapons issued up to date which were many and varied, such as Lewis machine-guns, flame throwers, ·300 American rifles, etc. The latter, encased in thick layers of grease caused much use of " old soldiers " language and our thoughts went back to the issue in 1915 of the Japanese carbines similarly preserved. However the job of cleaning was tackled with usual thoroughness and bright were the weapons, later to be proudly exhibited.

Musketry theoretical and practical were to be mastered first of all. The drill halls offered excellent covered accommodation for the instruction in aiming, etc., etc., whilst Kings' Playdown Range provided scope for firing practices up to 500 yards although it was impressed upon all that the shorter ranges were the most deadly in present day warfare. Many excellent N.C.O.s, some with Hythe School of Musketry experience, stepped forward to give nightly instruction, and months of very hard work resulted in a very sound knowledge of the weapons on hand.

In November, the Home Guard battalions in Wiltshire were numbered and we became the 4th Battalion Home Guard, the Wiltshire Regiment.

During the latter part of the year, the War Office instituted the War Office School for Home Guard Officers at Osterley Park, Middlesex, to which some of our officers went. On their return they were able to hand on the knowledge gained at the school to others, to the increased efficiency of the Battalion.

The spring of 1941 found the Battalion much better armed and uniformed whilst a great advance had been made in training. More men had come forward for enrolment and the Battalion strength was now 2,629 all ranks.

In February, commissions were granted to officers and the blue stripes, originally issued to denote leaders, were now replaced by the Regular Army insignia for officers.

In March it was decided to letter the companies instead of numbers, so that Nos. 1, 2, 3, 4 and 5 became " A ", " B ", " C ", " D " and " E " Companies respectively.

The month of May saw a change in the command of the Battalion as on the appointment of Brig.-Gen. Lord Roundway as Home Guard Commander for Wiltshire, Brig. G. Darwell, M.C., late the Border Regiment, took over the Battalion. " D " Company was therefore handed over to Lt.-Col. W. Walch, D.S.O., R.A. whilst the Battalion headquarters were moved to The Green Porch, Worton.

The importance of the Home Guard was rapidly increasing and a great deal of office work became essential, although higher authority promised otherwise. The job was becoming a full-time one and so the services of civilian clerks were authorised. One with years of Regular Army records experience was employed and the Battalion headquarters removed to Prince Hill, Worton where the increasing number of files, etc. could be more easily accommodated.

At this time also we welcomed our first Regular adjutant, Capt. E. A. Sandilands, the Royal Scots.

Recruits still came in and the Battalion strength increased. Many and varied were the weapons now issued, Browning machine-guns; Thompson sub-machine-guns, Browning Automatic Rifles, not to mention S.I. and grenades (68s and 36s) so that with these and also Northover Projectors and spigot mortars, there was a large armoury of weapons to be mastered.

To assist in the instruction on these weapons permanent staff instructors were sent from the Regular Army, Sgt.-Maj. Paget being first appointed to be joined later by Sgt.s Rhodes, Miness, Brady and S/Sgt.s Partridge and Dowding.

These instructors were allotted to certain companies whom they took under their wings. They did really sterling work in every phase of training.

To assist further in training, a travelling wing was sent out by the Denbies G.H.Q. Home Guard School. This consisted of specialist officers, W.O.s and N.C.O.s who could impart to their classes the very latest information on training matters ; they arranged small schemes and taught the latest subjects. It was always the policy of the Battalion Commander to have these wing programmes based on the subjects most required by the companies, and therefore, before a wing visited the Battalion, company commanders were asked to submit their requirements to Battalion Headquarters. These were invariably included in the following programme to the benefit and increased interest of all. These courses were very well attended and the knowledge gained later passed on to others.

Courses of instruction run on Regular Army lines, and staffed by Regular Army instructors, were established at Denbies, Woolacombe and Onibury. Many of our officers attended these most useful and interesting courses. It was therefore a natural result that the efficiency of the Battalion rapidly increased in subjects such as weapon training, patrolling, scouting, getting across country by night, rounding up paraproops and fieldcraft generally, together with much bombing and range practices.

Company and platoon exercises based on the existing rôle of the unit concerned were being continually carried out, and the force which had been born in such humble circumstances had become a most militant one.

The year 1942 saw many changes, chief among these being the introduction of compulsory enrolment of men between the ages of 17 and 51. This took place as from 16th February, but many months were to elapse before the labour exchanges were actually able to direct men to the various companies. To allow for this increase, the Battalion strength establishment was now fixed at 3,500, incidentally being the largest in the county. Three of the companies were fixed at 650 each and by the end of the year the actual strength of the Battalion was 106 officers and 2,920 other ranks, in other words, the strength of a brigade.

In May, on account of the age limit being strictly enforced, Maj. Walch, D.S.O. and Maj. Welchman, O.B.E. handed over command of " D " and " E " Companies to Vice-Admiral Tompkinson, C.B., M.V.O. and Maj. J. G. Walker, O.B.E. respectively.

Maj. Walch was later appointed Ammunition Officer in which capacity he gave most valuable service.

In July Capt. A. G. Smerdon, R.A. came to us as Quartermaster, performing the duties of A. & Q. of the Battalion right to the end of our existence as a Battalion headquarters, in September 1945. All ranks will remember with pleasure and gratitude, his work for us. Prior to his arrival R.Q.M.S. Pritchard had performed the none too easy task of issuing arms and equipment to the many scattered portions of the Battalion right from the formation of the unit.

The Battalion now held about 1,500 rifles and 500 Sten Guns, the successor to the Thompson which had been withdrawn for reissue to the Regular Army. Issues of all types of grenades continued and with a much increased scale of ammunition, ample opportunity was offered for practice especially during the long summer evenings.

In October, it was realised that some of the companies had reached unwieldy proportions, making them almost impossible for administration, supervision and training. It was therefore decided to form three new companies, namely " F ", " G " and " H ".

" F " Company was formed from the Bromham, Seend, Worton and Potterne Platoons from " D " Company, together with the Steeple Ashton Platoon from " A " Company. The Company was commanded by Maj. A. J. Fraser, M.C. with Capt. Power as Second in Command with headquarters at Seend.

" G " Company was formed from the Marden and Cannings Platoons from " D " Company with the addition of the Urchfont Platoon from " E " Company to be commanded by Maj. E. T. Carver with Capt. Moore as Second in Command, the headquarters being at Etchilhampton, but later removed to the Grange, Marden.

" H " Company commanded by Maj. J. M. Chrystal, M.C. with Capt. Ellis as Second in Command, took over the Bradford Platoons of " B " Company and established headquarters at Bradford-on-Avon.

In January 1943 Maj. Tompkinson and Capt. Ewart retired from " D " Company, and Maj. E. E. Copland Griffith's, who had previously been attached to Battalion Headquarters as Training Officer, took command of the Company with Capt. F. V. Weaver as his Second in Command.

Capt. E. H. Jellett, R.A., who had served since August 1939 on the headquarters staff of the 207th A.A. Training Regiment, R.A. in Devizes, and had consequently met many of the Battalion officers on " Blue Line " and other exercises, was posted to the Battalion as Adjutant, being mainly responsible for the training of the Battalion. Training programmes were soon to be arranged to cover all aspects of Home Guard training as directed and governed by the regular issue of Home Guard Instructions, normally G.H.Q. publications.

No indication had been given as to the possible use of gas by the enemy and so gas training had to be enforced. Capt. Brocklebank, R.N. was appointed Battalion Gas Officer. He inspected and reported on the gas training in the companies and organised a most useful Battalion course in this most important subject.

The Commanding Officer, always very keen to establish complete liaison with the civil authorities attended all civic conferences and a schedule was prepared and distributed showing names, addresses and telephone numbers of Battalion representatives on every invasion committee throughout the Battalion area, whether town, village or hamlet. This schedule was so complete that higher authority commented on its excellence and in fact urged other Home Guard battalions to prepare similar schedules.

It can safely be said with confidence that at all times there was complete cordiality between every unit of the Battalion, however small, and its civic counterpart. This spirit was also fostered by the organising of military-cum-civic schemes when problems were faced and solved to the benefit of all.

Early in 1943, the Battalion was included in a district exercise known as " Hawk ". This was a " message exercise ", messages being handed in by district officers, C.O., Adjutant, etc. to company or platoon headquarters at all times, and and to check the action theoretically taken. It was useful in its way and the Battalion came through well.

A system of " contact patrols " was so established throughout the Battalion area with definite contact points at regular intervals between dusk and dawn, that a complete network of patrols existed to calm the civil population in time of extreme anxiety and to keep all informed of any suspicious occurrence in the area.

A pigeon service between Bulford and Devizes was available but the great difficulty of feeding, etc. made the service impracticable.

The transport question had developed so much that it became increasingly difficult to distinguish between the various qualifications and their usage on " ACTION STATIONS ". It was therefore deemed advisable to make both lists of authorised, earmarked and " G " Licence cars tally, and by so doing, everyone knew that their car, on duty before an alarm was also on the " after alarm " list.

The old Territorial range at Semington was brought into use to meet the increased demand for musketry practices. This entailed extensive work being carried out. With this range in use, rifle range practices were greatly facilitated in the Battalion as there was a good range, duly renovated at Bradford-on-Avon, which accommodated " B " and " H " Companies, the range at Kings' Playdown accommodating ". D ", " E " and " G " Companies and the new Semington range to accommodate " A ", " C " and " F " Companies. Little wonder therefore that the skill at arms increased so throughout the Battalion.

During the summer, the Commanding Officer realised the need for a swift moving, strong body of men that he could call on at any time. He therefore formed a Battalion Mobile Reserve consisting of the Bromham Platoon. Lt. R. H. Angell was promoted to captain and commanded this force. The Adjutant, who had served in a cyclist unit in 1915, prepared a cyclist drill and this reserve very rapidly became a most valuable force, passing as they could through the countryside silently and rapidly to come into action at any point. This was actually demonstrated in a large district exercise later in the year, when they were so well handled by O.C. Melksham.

During the early part of the year the Battalion came under the control of Col. H. Burn, C.I.E. whose headquarters were at Corsham. Conferences were held at his headquarters, and he kept in contact with the Battalion most closely until the standing down. It was with very great pleasure that we always had Col. Burn's expert advice and help throughout his term of office. He was a constant visitor to our battle innoculation course.

On the 16th May we organised the first Battalion parade when all companies sent into Devizes strong contingents to make up a parade of just over 2,000. These came from about 20 village centres involving the use of 102 lorries. It was the first attempt at massing the Battalion and proved that, given three hours' notice, a concentration of the whole Battalion could be completed within two hours.

This parade provided the first opportunity to the dispatch riders for convoy work and they carried out the job excellently.

The Battalion marched past Brig.-Gen. Lord Roundway in the very unusual formation of " sixes " to meet the occasion of a massed Battalion parade. With the multiplicity of arms, and sub-artillery, etc., many were the surprised inhabitants who had only seen the Home Guard previously going to his place of parade in twos and threes.

This parade terminated with a thirteen minute demonstration of the Battalion Reserve wiping out an enemy strongpoint and very efficiently done it was too.

To bring the many operation instructions under one cover, the Commanding Officer issued in August his Battalion Operational Instruction. This proved to be Brig. Darwell's last effort as he shortly afterwards passed on very suddenly to the great regret of us all.

This order, printed and bound, was distributed to all concerned, about 250 copies being involved, and it can be truly said that it is a model in conciseness with rapid and easy reference to all information required in cases of emergency. Many were the favourable comments on the order received at Headquarters.

When the rôle of the Battalion became more aggressive as the war progressed in our favour, this order was amended to meet the requirements of the new rôle.

The actual issue of the order was noteworthy by the fact that it took place at the Town Hall, Melksham, when the large room was packed with all officers of the Battalion, about 130 being present. Probably this was the first and only time that all officers met, except at a " stand down " smoking concert on 1st Dec. 1944.

It was not long before the " Book of Words " was referred to as " WHITEHORSE " Exercise was staged by District as a very large scale operation, in which Regular troops took part and Melksham was directly concerned. At a District Commander's conference held later, it was stated that the Battalion had done very well and the exercise proved a great success.

During this summer, a very well worked out " Quick Decision Exercise " was staged by " E " Company covering all points of training including the intelligence staff. Excellent results were obtained. Had the Home Guard continued in being for the following summer, there is no doubt that this valuable form of exercise would have been repeated by other companies.

During the summer preparations were made for the " Bullets " Competition, an exercise that did so much to stimulate training and interest at a time when it was most needed. A cup was kindly presented by Messrs. Dotesio of Bradford-on-Avon for competition.

This scheme brought into operation the new battle drill, found to be so essential from experience gained in France when combating the new infiltration methods of the German spearhead. All platoons were taught this drill, at the same time preparing for the competition. Each company selected, by a process of elimination, the best platoon, and keen indeed was the spirit when on October 31st, the final was held at the Bradford-on-Avon Range. The feature of the competition was that all normal battle drill movements provided the foundation for leadership and markmanship with live ammunition. Penalties for training and drill faults were made and credit given for target hits and grenade throwing. The final score brought " C " Company to the top of the list and winners of the trophy.

Many air crashes occurred in the Battalion area with the result that a series of lectures were arranged in air crew rescue work. The main points to watch for the quick release of the air crews, were emphasised. Charts and actual equipment were demonstrated and it is noteworthy that many rescues were made by Home Guard personnel in the Battalion area.

The training of the Battalion Intelligence Sections had been under the care of Capt. Hon. C. H. Brassey, who by dint of continual rounds of duty, transformed this very important branch from small bands of guides, whose duties were the supply of all local information to any Regular troops passing through the area, to established sections of well trained personnel. These in many cases prepared maps of their localities covering such points as water supplies, bridge construction and head clearances, railway culverts, and even an up-to-date chart of moon rising and setting.

These sections were trained in map reading and field sketching and all aspects

71

of " I " work. The Intelligence Officer from District Headquarters visited the Battalion every month to lecture on current affairs, on Sundays. Exercises, especially when combined with the civil authorities gave the " I " sections full scope to prove their worth and a most efficient body of men were always at the disposal of company commanders.

These sections also proved the first link in the chain of liaison with the civil authorities, and the tact and diplomacy needed at times was never failing.

On the occasion of the visit to the Battalion by the newly appointed Director of Home Guard, Lord Bridgman, accompanied by the District Commander, Maj.-Gen. Curtis, a visit was made to the Trowbridge " I " Room. This room was the last word in efficiency and completeness. The visitors delayed their programme time schedule for their tour by a quarter of an hour so interested were they in this room and were heard to remark that the delay was well worth it. It was thought by some that the room was far too elaborate for practical purposes but this was proved false as on the occasion of the exercise " Jupiter " in which a full force of American troops were employed, the battle was handled excellently in this control room, much to the surprise of the American senior officers present. Church steeples, farm yokels, private and public telephones and a great deal of private " influence " all played their part in making this room a feature of Battalion intelligence training.

During the month of May, a pamphlet was issued governing the granting of proficiency badges and setting out the tests required to be passed. The standard set down was a very high one indeed, no fewer than six subjects had to be passed in which case a Commanding Officers certificate was granted and a record made in Orders. It can safely be said that even in the Regular Army the standard was not so high as required of these part-time soldiers.

Although at that time it was not so apparent, in the following spring it was most noticeable by everyone who saw the men on parade, that they had, by this winter training, made enormous steps towards efficiency in the highest degree. The candidates themselves admitted that the training for these tests arranged as it was, in stages, proved their most instructive and interesting period of their Home Guard service. Special convening orders and result sheets were prepared and printed exclusively for the Battalion.

Following the decease of Brig. Darwell, the command of the Battalion had remained vacant for several weeks although Sir Reginald Blake had kindly consented to " keep and eye on " documents etc., but expressed the view that his many public duties did not permit of his taking over the command. However, it was with great pleasure and satisfaction to all in the Battalion that after great persuasion by District, Sector and others, Sir Reginald finally agreed to command. He certainly always said afterwards that he took over command much against his will but it is also certain that he must have enjoyed the job very much to carry it out so well.

Conferences were held as hitherto every month and complete cordiality existed between Comanding Officer, Headquarter Staff and company Commanders. points were settled round the table and a very happy feeling grew amongst all.

In January 1944 Battalion Headquarters previously at Worton removed to Spa Road, Melksham being more central to the Battalion area and furthermore nearer Corsham Sector Headquarters. This accommodation, however, proved inadequate to all branches of the staff and a further removal to " Giffords ", Lowbourne, Melksham, took place a few months later. An excellent layout was provided for security governed staff rooms, control room, intelligence, signals, despatch riders, together with sleeping accommodation in case of a prolonged " stand to," whilst the monthly or emergency conferences were also held there. The outbuildings accommodated the multitudinous headquarters stores and spares.

The Battalion Despatch Riders, hitherto practically untrained, had by this time worked on a carefully prepared schedule of training, providing alternate Sundays in theoretical and practical work. Great keenness was shown, they became to know not only the Battalion area intimately but also routes to adjoining battalion headquarters, Sector and District Headquarters, etc. Furthermore on " action stations " one or more of our D.R.s immediately reported for duty to Headquarters Sector at Corsham.

Maj. A. J. Fraser, M.C. was appointed Second in Command of the Battalion and his advice on all matters together with the great amount of work he put in was most appreciated by all at Headquarters. His company, " F " was taken over by Capt. R. H. Angell, promoted to major, and the Mobile Reserve was taken over by Lt. H. Angell.

On 21st May, 1944 the second birthday parade was organised, this time at Trowbridge when 75 officers and 1,609 other ranks paraded. They were transported by American vehicles of all types. Forming up took place on the playing fields of the High School, the salute being taken by Gen. Dager of the U.S.A. Army. The parade, led by the band of the Royal Artillery, and supplemented by the band of " D " Company marched through Trowbridge to the Park. The whole Mobile Reserve and D.R.s completed the parade.

The following month was to provide the greatest expedition in our history since the days of Drake and Raleigh—now known as " D " Day. With our troops operating against the coast of Normandy, it was thought possible that the enemy would engage in counter moves by dropping paratroops to sabotage railways, factories, etc. Battalion and Company Headquarters were manned day and night until the danger period had passed and this again gave a new interest to all. Guards were detailed whose duty it was to patrol the many railway bridges throughout the area, thus directly contributing to the success of the overseas operations. The men felt that they were doing a useful job of work, great keeness was shown and many were the night intruders brought in by these guards for failing to answer challenges, etc. An official from the War Office making a special visit to the area, on a May morning at 02.00 hrs. expressed surprise at the keenness and efficiency of these guards. Battalion Headquarters were manned day and night during the months of May and June.

The war had by now taken a definite turn in our favour, the Home Guard began to see no further need for training, parades were dropping off, and it seemed that at along last, prosecutions would have to be resorted to. Something had to be done about it and the answer was found in the magic words " battle innoculation ".

A course ideally suited for the purpose, was found within the Battalion area and when completed furnished the most excellent training possible. The N.C.O.s and men had an opportunity at last of carrying out in practice all they had learned during the long winter months.

The course was visited regularly by the Sector Commander, District Headquarters staff officers, Regular unit officers, neighbouring Home Guard Battalion Commanders and a host of others who all expressed admiration of such an excellent form of training.

The course consisted of an uphill valley between downland rising from 600 to 700 feet. At the further end of the course, was a central wooded gulley. The object was to accustom the men to battle noises, attain steadiness under battle conditions and to stimulate interest in training. A normal squad under its own leader would, on arrival, and out of sight of the course, be briefed as to details, would then form up in line in battle order with bayonets fixed and proceed up the course at a steady pace under the command of the squad commander.

All types of targets (Figs. 2, 3, 4a and 5) were engaged at ranges of from a few feet to 300 yards, and the types of firing comprised deliberate, hip, kneeling, standing, prone, aiming off and snap, and in addition both rising and ground dummies provided bayonet work.

The running target across the full width of the course was also a feature.

The companies were called upon at odd times to undertake varied duties of a ceremonial nature such as Guards of Honour, National Savings Week parades, etc., etc., and a very important duty fell on " D " Company, namely, escorting the late Brig.-Gen. Lord Roundway to his resting place. Owing to the absence of Regular troops now in Normandy, this duty was carried out without rehearsal, the unusual musical items being provided by the Company's band. The Slow March, never before executed by the men, and the many other strange items of ceremonial drill (not permitted to be taught in the Home Guard) were taken in their stride, and the performance they put up was most creditable.

September saw the cessation of compulsory enrolment to the Home Guard.

November brought the first and only officers' competition in the form of revolver shooting at the battle innoculation course. The practices included application, timed, snap rising and snap moving. Lt. Davie (54) and Lt. Harris-Burland (52) both of " D " Company being winner and runner-up respectively.

December saw the " Stand down " of the Home Guard and the commencement of a round of social functions to celebrate the occasion. Dinners and dances took place throughout the Battalion area and many were the yarns swapped.

Our numbers were now 135 officers and 2,920 other ranks, totalling 3,055, the strongest battalion in the county.

On December 3rd the " Stand down " Parade was held at Trowbridge when the May arrangements were successfully repeated except that on this occasion the

74

parade was led by the band of the Royal Artillery, Salisbury Plain District supplemented by the band of "D" Company. 107 officers and 1,365 other ranks paraded. The salute was taken by Col. H. Burn, C.I.E., the Western Sector Commander, who before the dispersal included in his farewell message, his congratulations on the work put in by the Battalion.

On December 1st there was organised, on a somewhat amusing operation order, a gathering of all Battalion officers at a "smoker" in Devizes Drill Hall, when the Revolver Competition trophy was presented to the winner.

Also on December 3rd the Battalion was honoured by supplying the Commander of the units of the Wiltshire and Dorset Contingent at the Hyde Park Home Guard Standing Down Parade, Maj. E. E. Copland Griffiths taking command and the Battalion sending three other ranks.

Since the "Stand down", old comrades associations have been formed and the comradeship of the Battalion is being happily preserved. Rifle clubs are established and it is pleasing to note that the excellent standard of musketry through the Battalion is reflected in the fact that the Battalion has recently won the Lord Lieutenant's Cup open to all Home Guard Battalions in the county. Furthermore, of other trophies offered and competed for at the recent County Rifle Meeting on Kings' Playdown Range, representatives of the Battalion secured the Cup for the highest aggregate, the Gold Medal open to the county, the cup open to non ex-servicemen, and Dr. Gibson, the Battalion Medical Officer showed his prowess by runner-up for the Veteran's Cup. This was practically a "sweep the board" effort and congratulations are due to all who participated.

In conclusion, it may confidently be stated that, although the Home Guard as conceived appeared but a feeble child, very few had the slightest idea that in a very short time, it would develop into a young man well able to look after the country in times of emergency and thus release the Regular troops for service overseas, contributing so much to the final victory of our armies.

5TH BATTALION WILTSHIRE HOME GUARD

THE 5th Battalion was originally formed following a suggestion by Rear Admiral Hyde Parker who called upon the Mayor of Swindon soon after Mr. Anthony Eden's famous appeal. A meeting was called by the Mayor (the late Mr. H. Hustings) during May 1940 at which those present included the Mayor, Rear Admiral Hyde Parker, Lt.-Col. Birley, D.S.O., Mr. J. B. L. Thompson, M.C., and Mr. D. Murray John (Town Clerk).

At the initial meeting Lt.-Col. Birley was asked to take command and he appointed the following officers :

Second in Command	J. B. L. Thompson
Adjutant	Rev. L. A. Erett
Quartermaster	L. F. Cheyney (Borough Treasurer)
Musketry Officer	M. Cuss

After the appointment of headquarter officers the following appointments to command certain areas were made :

Area—Great Western Railway	S. Dyer
,, Gas Works	C. H. Chester
,, Electricity Power Station	A. E. Beswick
,, South of Swindon	J. C. Gilbert
,, H.Q. Company	S. Hirst

Within a few days areas and companies were rearranged as follows :

Coy.	Areas	Commanders
1	Electricity Power Station	A. E. Beswick
2	Gas Works	C. H. Chester
3	Great Western Railway	S. Dyer
4	Garrard's Factory	H. V. Slade
5	South-west	Dr. C. E. Jones
6	Western	W. E. Russell, M.C.
7	South-eastern	J. C. Gilbert
8	H.Q. Company	S. Hirst
9	Post Office Company	T. Fenner

At this time the Battalion was known as the Local Defence Volunteers and the Headquarters were at the Civic Offices with a room in the basement for Q.M. stores. Mr. R. C. Budding supervised the issue of all items of stores, being chief assistant to the Quartermaster. Mr. Budding put in a tremendous amount of hard work and under difficult circumstances then prevailing carried out his duties very efficiently. He was not like a typical army Quartermaster, he issued equipment with celerity as fast as it arrived. Thanks to the willing co-operation of the Swindon Education Committee and the Swindon Corporation a number of schools were assigned as company headquarters in the various areas which were used in the evenings and on Sunday mornings for parades and lectures.

The following were the original headquarters of the various companies :

No. 1 Rodbourne Schools
,, 2 Canteen Buildings—Gorse Hill Gas Works and Gorse Hill Schools
,, 3 Great Western Railway Works
,, 4 The Garrard Engineering and Manufacturing Company Factory
,, 5 The Commonweal School
,, 6 The County Ground Hotel and Queenstown School
,, 7 The Lethbridge Road Schools
,, 8 The Clarence Street Schools
,, 9 The Post Office

Each company commander raised his own company and volunteers came in by hundreds and within a few days of the formation of companies, guards were mounted every evening at all the approaches to the town. At the beginning it was impossible to arrange proper reliefs and in many instances the same men were on duty all night—in fact at this time it was not unusual for men to do guard duty three nights during the week.

All cars and pedestrians were challenged, identity papers examined. Many stories are unprintable but the following is claimed to be quite true :

" In the ' wee sma" ' hours the guard at the approach in the Old Town collected a man very intoxicated and quite incapable. While a member of the guard was endeavouring to find ways and means of getting the man to his home, the incapable one fell asleep on the side of the road, face downwards, arms spread outwards. A car containing an apoplectic gentleman was stopped who produced his identity card after considerable pressure all the time passing jeering remarks about the Local Defence Volunteers. On being informed that the guard's rifle was loaded he said, ' In any case you'd be too windy to fire the damn thing.' The guard, pointing to the prone one said, ' What about him ? ' The car drove off at a furious speed while the occupant muttered, ' It's rank murder.' "

Weapon state at this time was very bad. Gen. Sir F. Gathorne Hardy who had taken command of the North Wiltshire Local Defence Volunteer Zone was able to obtain the loan of some rifles from Marlborough College, and these were distributed among the companies in the proportion of about fifteen per company. The weapon state remained unsatisfactory until June 1941 when rifles from America arrived.

By 23 July 1940, when a speech by Mr. Winston Churchill turned the Local Defence Volunteers into the Home Guard, the Swindon Battalion was about fifteen hundred strong and reached its maximum strength in April 1943 when the strength of the Battalion was over two thousand.

During the early days companies tried to improve their fighting strength by the manufacture of hundreds of Molotov bombs known as Molotov Cocktails, hundreds of bottles of all shapes and sizes were used for this purpose. Gradually the weapon state improved by the arrival of American Lewis Guns and these were assigned roughly four to each company. By the end of May 1944 the Battalion was well armed with rifles, Sten Guns, grenades, Northover Projectors, spigot mortars, Smith Guns and 2-pounder anti-tank guns, and at the time of the stand down on the 1st November 1944 had 3,000 weapons of all kinds.

At the end of 1942 Maj. Thompson, the Second in Command of the Battalion. resigned, and Maj. A. E. Beswick was appointed Second in Command, and on 12th March 1943 Lt.-Col. Birley, owing to reasons of health, resigned, and Maj. A. E. Beswick was appointed to command the Battalion with the rank of Lt.-Col. On 1st May 1943 No. 3. Company now known as " F " Company consisting of 17 officers and 623 other ranks was transferred from the 5th Battalion to form the nucleus of another battalion to be known as the 13th Battalion, and was commanded by its former Company Commander, Maj. Dyer with the rank of Lt.-Col. In the autumn of 1942 the Rocket A.A. Battery was formed in the Swindon area and was at first affiliated to the 5th Battalion and later to all Battalions of the Swindon area and over 600 men were transferred from the 5th to the Rocket Battery.

During March 1943 a competent Adjutant was appointed in the person of Capt. E. J. Dyball of the K.R.R.C., and later in addition Capt. H. C. Hewett of The Buffs was appointed Quartermaster and two excellent P.S.I.s, Sgt.-Maj. Avent and Sgt.-Maj. Coombs.

It was also necessary to increase the civilian staff at Battalion Headquarters, and at the time of the stand down of the Home Guard the paid civilian staff consisted of Miss Macphearson, Mrs. Turner and Mrs. Honeyman, a very happy combination of excellent assistants. During 1943 more room was required, and it was necessary to move Battalion Headquarters to larger offices at 45 Regent Street, Swindon.

The 5th Battalion at the end of 1944 had a very well organised headquarters, consisting of a competent Battalion signals section complete with wireless equipment and a pigeon service (attached to N.E. Section), intelligence section, transport and ammunition officers, Press officer, medical officer, liaison officer and a very fine military band under the able direction of Bandmaster Wood. By this time also many changes had taken place as the following list of company commanders and headquarter staff will show :

Commanding Officer	Lt.-Col. A. E. Beswick, O.B.E.
Second in Command	Maj. W. H. Liebow
Adjutant	Capt. E. J. Dyball, K.R.R.C.
A./Q. Officer	Capt. H. C. Hewett, The Buffs
Medical Officer	Maj. O. B. Pratt, M.B.
Liaison Officer	Capt. D. H. Maclean
Signals Officer	Lt. W. Wheeler
Intelligence Officer	Lt. R. J. Naish
Ammunition Officer	Lt. H. Williams
Transport Officer	Lt. C. H. How

Companies

"H.Q." Company, Capt. R. C. Budding ; "A" Company, Maj. W. E. Russell, M.C., Headquarters, The Hutments, Dudmore Road, Swindon ; "B" Company, Maj. W. E. G. Ireland, Headquarters, Commonweal School, Swindon ; "C" Company, Maj. C. H. Gilbert, Headquarters, Hutments, Gipsy Lane, Swindon ; "D" Company, Maj. E. Blewitt, Headquarters, G.P.O., Swindon ; "E" Company Maj. Parrett, Headquarters, Garrard's Engineering Works ; "G" Company, Maj. P. S. Richards, M.B.E., Headquarters, Rodbourne Cheney Schools ; "H" Company, Maj. W. N. Knight, Headquarters, Works Depot, Swindon ; "J" Company, Maj. W. H. Haydon, Headquarters, Drill Hall, Swindon.

During the early days of the Battalion it came under the direction of several high ranking officers. Gen. Gathorne Hardy, G.C.B., G.C.V.O., D.S.O., being the first Zone Commander, Lt.-Col. Eddie Campbell of the K.R.R.s who commanded a training unit at Chiseldon, Col. Hamilton, Brig.-Gen. Lord Roundway who succeeded Gen. Gathorne Hardy as Zone Commander, Lt.-Col. R. H. Broom who was officially training officer and was the 1st Sector Commander and who was extremely helpful and popular with all ranks. The Battalion also received several visits from Maj.-Gen. Curtis, C.B., D.S.O., M.C., who was Commanding Officer of Salisbury Plain District and also later Maj.-Gen. Laurie, C.B., C.B.E., who afterwards succeeded him. At the time of the stand down Col. Wilson Fitzgerald, D.S.O., M.C., was Sector Commander.

In the early dangerous days Col. Hamilton of Sub-Area Headquarters spent a lot of time in Swindon, greatly to the benefit of the Battalion.

During the active life of the Battalion several interesting and instructive exercises were carried out. The " Jupiter " exercise in September 1942 under the direction of Col. Hamilton of Sub-Area Headquarters being probably the most instructive, when the Battalion was under arms for two days and feeding arrangements were exercised and carried out individually by companies. On this occasion the attacking force was the M.T. Battalion, K.R.R.s.

On 16th May 1943 a large Home Guard anniversary parade was arranged in Swindon when all the battalions in the area participated. Maj.-Gen. H. O. Curtis, C.B., D.S.O.; M.C., took the salute and afterwards the Commanding Officer of the 5th Battalion had the pleasure of entertaining all the battalion commanders, the Mayor and Town Clerk of Swindon and Maj.-Gen. Curtis and his staff to lunch. On this occasion the 5th Battalion, after the parade, put on a very effective display of street fighting.

At this time the Battalion was at its most effective strength and training and the standard was afterwards never higher owing to the compulsory transfers of the best men to the newly formed A.A. Battery. Other important parades were 14th May 1944 when Maj.-Gen. Laurie took the salute, in which the 5th Battalion Band was at full strength, the Stand-down Parade when Maj.-Gen. Laurie, C.B., C.B.E. took the salute and the Thanksgiving Parade and church service when the Sector Commander, Col. Wilson Fitzgerald, D.S.O., M.C., took the salute, the service being conducted by the Vicar of Rodbourne Cheney Parish Church, the Rev. Heath, a good friend.

As the late Army Commander, Southern Command and now in command in the London district truly said, " The success of the Home Guard was founded on goodwill."

The great help and co-operation of the Wiltshire County Territorial Associations contributed largely to the success of the 5th Battalion.

Mention should also be made to the first camp at Castle Eaton during August and September 1943 which was a great success.

6TH WILTSHIRE BATTALION HOME GUARD

THE Battalion came into existence as a result of a public meeting held in Marlborough in May, 1940, following the appeal for Local Defence Volunteers. Among those attending was Gen. Sir Francis Gathorne Hardy, organiser for the County of Wiltshire and Zone Commander of the Local Defence Volunteers, and who throughout was to be so closely associated with the Marlborough Battalion.

Similar meetings were held in the surrounding parishes and the response was immediate and almost overwhelming. An organisation, which was to become the 6th Wiltshire Battalion, Home Guard was set up to co-ordinate the activities of the Local Defence Volunteers in an area comprising Marlborough and the Marlborough and Ramsbury Rural District with the addition of Burbage. It might appear unnecessary to set down the story of this call to arms, resulting from the expectation of invasion, so closely does it resemble the accounts of the time when Napoleon made invasion appear an equal certainty. In both cases the Government appealed for volunteers, in both the appeal was answered in such fashion that it was quite impossible to provide the necessary arms, in both, pikes were offered as an alternative. But if the broad outlines are identical, with the hour producing the man, and the spirit of the people unchanged, invention and the passage of years had altered conditions and what was required of the volunteers.

Time was not on our side, and improvisation was the order of the day. The Battalion had to go on duty and sort itself out as it went. Through all the rush and scramble of the early weeks ; collecting and distributing whatever rifles or shotguns became available, caps and Local Defence Volunteer armlets ; passing on directives, orders and counter-orders ; conferences with " Striking Force ", District Command and other military formations ; co-operation with the neighbouring battalions, with the Police and Civil Defence ; enrolling and sorting out the rush of volunteers, digging trenches and weapon pits, fitting denim overalls, doing duty at the road-blocks and O.P.s, arranging elementary training and instruction ; through all this the Battalion settled towards its final shape and a strength of 1,800 officers and men.

With Battalion Headquarters in Marlborough, where was also the Zone Commanders Headquarters, there evolved H. Q. Wing, including Transport, Intelligence, Signals and " Q ", each with their specialists, " A " Company of seven platoons, and for a time " E " Company. There were detachments from Marlborough College and from the City of London School, and a platoon of Post Office employees, whilst the air raid wardens, answering a call for additional strength to man the " Tank Island ", joined the Home Guard and trained regularly in addition to carrying out their Civil Defence duties. Outside the Borough boundary were three companies, the company areas containing up to twenty scattered villages and hamlets.

" B " Company with Headquarters at Lockeridge and platoons with platoon headquarters at Ogbourne St. George, Ogbourne St. Andrew, Manton Down, Lockeridge, Overton, Beckhampton, Avebury, Winterbourne Bassett and Broad Hinton.

" C " Company with Headquarters at Aldbourne and platoons at Aldbourne, Ramsbury, Chilton Foliat and Baydon.

" D " Company, with Headquarters at Shalbourne and later at Wilton, and platoon headquarters at Wilton, Great Bedwyn, Little Bedwyn, Shalbourne, Ham, Fosbury, Burbage and Savernake.

The strength of platoons varied from about 30 to as many as 60-90 in the larger villages. Women assisted their local units as clerks, telephonists, drivers, camp cooks, etc., whilst the first aid posts were prepared to look after their casualties.

In the tense summer of 1940, when it was known that first news of the attempted invasion might be an announcement on the wireless at any moment of the twenty-four hours, women took turns to sit up through the night by the silent but switched-on wireless, whilst their men-folk watched the countryside for parachutists.

During the struggles of its early existence, with only a handful of individuals able to give their whole time, and the vast majority working overtime at their civil occupation, the rôle of the Local Defence Volunteers was to hold Marlborough and a number of villages as " centres of resistance ", to delay the expected enemy advance. There was much planning of defences for Marlborough and the " defended villages ", as well as for the " Blue Line "—a defence line alone the Kennett and Avon Canal in the holding of which " D " Company were to be employed between Burbage and Froxfield. To strengthen these positions, many concrete " pill boxes " and tank obstructions were erected.

Whilst preparing for this rôle, the Local Defence Volunteers were called upon for duty at the road-blocks and O.P.s

At a few hours notice, orders would be received to check up on all travellers that night, and sometimes there would be added the detailed description of some wanted suspect. Somehow the word would be passed round and arrangements made for farm wagons, rails and what-not to form a block, and red lamps to warn the traffic, and at dusk Local Defence Volunteers would assemble at some twenty points in the Battalion area. Many men had not enrolled until they presented themselves at the road-block and were handed a cap and a Local Defence Volunteer armlet. One in ten would be given a rifle and five rounds, one or two others, a shotgun.

Within five minutes of being enrolled they were on duty, with an ex-serviceman to give some sort of shape to the collection of individuals and to direct some more or less formal procedure. The men had been working all day and some had to be milking by 5 a.m. the next morning—there was no guard room in which to shelter or rest, and perhaps the blocks were some miles from where they lived. In such cases, the summer night would be divided into two four hours of duty, and private car owners, men and women, would transport the first section to the block at 9 p.m., bring the relief and return the first section at 1 a.m., and fetch home the relief at 5 a.m. In June and July 1940, there were three continuous weeks of this, to be followed by the manning of the observation posts—with training and trench digging and the growing pains to be contended with as well. If expenditure of energy and lack of sleep are the yardstick, that was perhaps the hey-day of the Local Defence Volunteers, and there were laid the foundations for the hey-day of the Home Guard later on.

There were some thirty O.P.s in the Battalion area, for the most part, of course, high up on the tops of the Downs. How often, long centuries ago, must sentinels have stood watch, at these same vantage points, over our heritage in its infancy.

For months the Local Defence Volunteers and Home Guard kept watch from these O.P.s for enemy parachutists, from them they saw distant flashes or a glow in the sky as London or Bristol suffered in the " blitz ", and the occasional bombs which fell aimlessly across the countryside.

Although the regular manning of these O.P.s was eventually discontinued, they would all have been occupied in the event of the Home Guard being mustered— the one constant factor in their operational rôle being the passing of quick and accurate information of enemy activity to higher formations.

All this while, training parades were developing, Sunday mornings were a fixture and usually one evening per week with instruction provided according to its availability. Gradually the rush and improvisation of the early days gave place to strictly regulated training and more expert instruction, more and more closely the Army took part in the guidance and training of the Home Guard, and officers and N.C.O.s were seconded for permanent duty with the Home Guard.

The Local Defence Volunteers had become the Home Guard and in 1941 officers were given Home Guard commissions in their respective grades.

To the regret of many, conscription took place of the voluntary effort, but in reality the force was still dependant on the latter. Step by step fully equipped and well armed platoons were to supersede the band of almost unarmed men, half a dozen varieties of grenades displaced the " Molotov cocktail ", and the " Northover Projector " became as out-moded at the shotgun.

Weapon training instead of being confined to the rifle was to involve a variety to strain the capacity of these part time soldiers. Instead of being fortunate if he shared a rifle with only one other man, the Home Guard was to be provided with cup-dischargers, machine-guns of several types, Sten Guns, spigot mortars, 2-pounder anti-tank guns, Smith Guns and an ever growing number of grenades. Time had to be found for map-reading, and protection against gas, and signallers were taught to use portable wireless sets. He was expected to become proficient in the use of the rifle and one other weapon and to know something of them all.

Instead of forming fours he was expected to master the elaborate procedure of squad and platoon battle drill.

It says much surely for the manner in which these hard-worked men—(and some had not had a day's holiday, Sundays included, since the war began)— tackled their task, that a Regular officer should have described a demonstration of

83

platoon battle drill, as being up to the standard of men who had had six month's training in the Army.

The Battalion were fortunate in being allowed to use the Marlborough College rifle ranges and many of the rural platoons by their own labour and at their own expense, provided ranges for themselves. A competition at Perham Down open to the Home Guard of two counties was won by a team from the 6th Wiltshire Battalion from thirty-one competitors, and when definite range practices were laid down for the purpose, a very creditable number qualified for their marksman's badge.

As the possibility of an enemy sea-borne invasion receded, the emphasis which had been laid on " centres of resistance " and static defence generally—such as the Canal Line, was changed to that of a more mobile rôle, and only Marlborough itself was still a " tank island " to be defended at all costs. The vast ammunition dump in Savernake Forest added to the responsibilities of the Battalion and brought them into close co-operation with U.S. troops. The platoons were to be prepared for enemy airborne landings and to be practiced in moving quickly to harass or destroy them. And so through the years and the fluctuating fortunes of war, all ranks with changing rôle and unchanged enthusiasm, pursued their training and performed their daily tasks. Working it is true, from the blessed comfort of their unblitzed homes, aided and abetted by their women-folk, men did the work of two men, preparing for the battle that was not to be.

For a considerable period they put in three parades a week, and the officers four. Routine training and weapon practices were interspersed with lectures and T.E.W.T.s ; with proficiency tests, with exercises by day and exercises by night ; with exercises that might involve two platoons or several battalions and co-operation with the Army, the Civil Defence Services and the Police ; with demonstrations and competitions ; with an occasional Battalion parade and march past in Marlborough High Street ; with week-end or longer courses of instruction ; with an occasional church parade and the unaccustomed tonic of an overflowing church ; or a week-end in the Battalion camp at Winterbourne Bassett.

The carrying out of this programme in addition to routine administration, involved all concerned in a great deal of labour in the way of preparation alone, despite all that was done by Army officers and N.C.O.s attached to the Battalion. The company and platoon commanders, the Quartermaster, and the officers in charge of Transport, Signals and Intelligence may well have felt that their work was never done, and it has been suggested that their names should be included in these notes. It is felt, however, that to do this would be contrary to the spirit in which men did their best in whatever rank they were called upon to serve, and that these officers would not wish to be publicised to the exclusion of the many who assisted them so loyally in less conspicuous appointments and in the ranks.

The nominal roll and the record of service lie in the office of the County Territorial Association, which worked so closely and in such harmony with the Home Guard as it fulfilled its considerable tasks of equipment, accounting and records.

The Battalion received its strictly limited ration of Certificates of Good Service, an M.B.E., and on two occasions the B.E.M. was awarded to N.C.O.s who by their coolness and disregard of personal danger, prevented casualties when mishaps occurred on the bombing range.

As " D " Day approached, there returned a period of night duty, to watch over vital points on the railway and the enormous supply dump that was established on the roads leading into Aldbourne. But long since, the Battalion had made its nearest approach to hostilities that it was ever destined to make. Back in the early days, the Battalion closely assembled on Barton Down for a demonstration by the R.A.F., and instruction in aiming at enemy aircraft, was seen by a German plane which dropped two bombs, but they fell so wide of their mark that most present thought it was a part of the demonstration.

And when it was clear that there would now be no enemy attacks on this country, all duties and parades were cancelled and anti-climax followed the four and a half years toil.

On 3rd, December 1944, the Battalion assembled in Marlborough for its " Stand down " Parade and sent representatives to the ceremony in London. After a service in St. Mary's, Gen. Sir Francis Gathorne Hardy took the salute in the High Street and addressed the parade. The Mayor and Corporation were at the saluting base, and after the Mayor and the Commanding Officer had spoken, the Battalion marched off to its far-scattered homes and was no more seen.

There remained to carry out the final instructions, " All arms, ammunition and equipment to be returned to store, boots and uniforms to be retained." Posterity will say what was done with all the good fellowship, unselfishness and unity of purpose, so needed, now that the war was ended, to put an end to war.

7TH BATTALION WILTSHIRE HOME GUARD

A SHORT history of the 7th Battalion Wiltshire Home Guard has been compiled so that all ranks may have in their possession a memento of their service during four critical years. I hope that it will also remind them of the good comradeship that existed, and long may it remain.

GEOFFREY BROOKE,
Maj.-Gen.

Christmas 1944.

HISTORY OF THE 7TH (SALISBURY) BATTALION

ON 23rd May 1940, the 7th (Salisbury) Battalion Wiltshire Local Defence Volunteers was formed under the direction of Maj.-Gen. Walter Hill, C.B., C.M.G., D.S.O., whose official title at that time was Group Organiser. The Battalion covered the whole Amesbury Police District, including Salisbury City, and consisted of five companies, viz., Amesbury Company (under Lt.-Col. R. Stephens), Wilton Company (under Brig. T. O. Seagram, C.M.G., D.S.O.), Downton Company (under the Earl of Essex), Alderbury Company (under Maj. W. M. J. Martin), and the City of New Sarum Company (under Maj.-Gen. H. G. B. Freeth, C.B., C.M.G., D.S.O.

Plans were also made for a Local Defence Mobile Reserve to be raised in Salisbury by Maj.-Gen. Geoffrey Brooke, C.B., D.S.O., M.C. This reserve was originally known as the Sarum City Mobile Reserve, but, on the formation of the City of New Sarum Company into the 8th Battalion Wiltshire Home Guard the reserve which stayed with the 7th Battalion, became known as the Mobile Column. In July, Gen. Hill became Battalion Commander and Maj. A. E. Phillips, D.S.O., Assistant Battalion Commander, and Maj. Martin handed over command of Alderbury Company to Maj.-Gen. Sir Henry Everett, C.B., K.C.M.G. During the summer the speed of growth varied greatly in different localities and it was soon clear that a number of redistributions would have to take place. The first took place in October, when the New Sarum Company broke away and became the 8th Battalion Wiltshire Home Guard.

An Important Area

The position of Amesbury Company was also under consideration. The strength of this company was over 700, and the Amesbury contingent, with a strength of 110, ranked as a section. This area was split up into Amesbury Company (comprising Amesbury and the villages in Avon and Bourne Valleys) and Shrewton Company (comprising Shrewton, Winterbourne Stoke and Durrington) under the command of Brig. O. S. Cameron, D.S.O. The Battalion area was considered very important and also very vulnerable owing to the large stretches of open plain. The major operational rôles assigned were to watch and report enemy airborne landings, and to delay the enemy at specified road-blocks.

Observation posts, which were continuously manned at night, were therefore established at commanding points, and much work was done on the layout of road-blocks. The obstructions were for the most part home made, because the only stores provided by the Army were a small quantity of Dannert and barbed wire. Much ingenuity was shown in towing broken-down cars and lorries, oil drums, barrels, farm carts and so on, and anything else that might delay the enemy's advance.

Training concentrated mainly around these road-blocks. There could be, and was, very little central control of training. At each road-block the men paraded again and again in order that the road-block commander could try out a variety of methods in defence. A little shooting was done, but weapons and arms were in short supply. Large numbers of " Molotov Cocktails " were filled, some being flung against improvised tanks and others being stored. Shotguns were still in use as a major armament.

The Mobile Column was then organised as a cavalry unit with two squadrons consisting of four troops—" A " Squadron based on the Anna Valley and Wessex Garages, both of whom provided cars, " B " Squadron being drawn in the same way from Goddards Garrage and the Salisbury Steam Laundry. The troops were known as Anna Valley, Wessex, Goddards and Laundry Troops. The column, therefore, had the distinction of containing the only laundry troop that has ever existed in the British Army.

An ambulance unit, Wiltshire 5, B.R.C.S., was also attached, under the command of Commandant C. H. Harris, M.B.E. The eminent London specialist, Dr. R. Foster Moore, O.B.E., became Column Medical Officer, so that the unit was remarkably well placed to deal with casualties.

On the nights of 7th-8th September there was an alarm and Home Guards throughout England stood to. Within the hour 80 per cent of the Battalion were fully mustered throughout the 500 square miles of the Battalion area, a feat which rightly earned high praise from Brig. Fleming, O.B.E., M.C., the Sub-Area Commander.

About Two Thousand

At the beginning of 1941 the Battalion consisted of five companies, comprising nineteen platoons and the Mobile Column, the total strength of the Battalion being around 2,000. In January owing to ill-health, Gen. Hill gave up command, and Maj. A. E. Phillips, D.S.O., became Battalion Commander, being gazetted Lt.-Col. on 1st February 1941. However, Gen. Hill continued to act as honorary colonel.

No sub-division of companies was made but in October Downton Company was split into two operational commands, Downton Defences being placed under Lt.-Col. Tarleton, D.S.O., whilst Coombe Bissett Defences remained under the Company Commander, Lord Essex.

Battalion H.Q. was increased by the appointment of Capt. R. B. Carrow on 7th, April to be Adjutant and Quartermaster, and of Sgt. T. E. Davies on 15th July to be Permanent Staff Instructor. Home Guard appointments to Battalion H.Q. were Col. H. C. Travers, C.B.E., D.S.O., to be Battalion Ammunition Officer with the rank of lieutenant, and Dr. J. C. Mathews, M.C., to be Battalion Medical Officer, with the rank of major.

The operational rôle continued to be centred in road-blocks and observation posts. The Mobile Column was given a mixed reconnaissance and fighting rôle in the Battalion area, south of River Nadder and Railway, Salisbury—Southampton to southern edge of Battalion boundary.

In the early part of the year the first attempt at centralised training was made when Battalion H.Q. ran a series of three week-end schools at Bulford. These schools were also attended by Home Guards from the 3rd and 8th Battalions. But training continued to grow both in numbers and scope. Weapons were being issued more liberally and by the end of the year about 50 per cent of the Battalion had rifles. Ammunition was still scarce but some practice was carried out. Stickies (74s), and Mills grenades (36s) were issued and about half the Battalion went at various times to the Bulford grenade range. The first L.M.G.s were issued and also the first Northovers. A discreet veil is drawn over the issue of pikes and bludgeons.

New Company Commanders

Superannuations being enforced, Maj. Seagram handed over Wilton Company to Lord Pembroke, and Maj.-Gen. Sir Henry Everett handed over Alderbury Company to Lt.-Col. D. D. Haskard, M.C. Lt.-Col. A. E. Phillips, whose services had previously been extended to April, 1942, received further extension to the end of the year. Brig. Cameron became Battalion Second in Command, handing over Shrewton Company to Maj. P. W. F. Elderkin. In June, Capt. F. B. Landale, M.C., was appointed Battalion Quartermaster, and Maj. F. R. Way, O.B.E., took command of the newly formed 2142 M.T. Company. In October Porton and Winterbourne Gunner were detached from " A " Company and became the Bourne Valley Company under Maj. Garnett. The Nadder Valley Platoon also left the Wilton Company and became the Nadder Valley Company under Maj. Woolley.

The official " ceiling " for the Battalion was fixed at 2,187 excluding the M.T. Company, but this figure was soon reached and passed. Operationally, static defence went somewhat out of fashion and the emphasis fell on mobility. Mobile or fighting patrols were constituted at all defended localities. Great interest was taken in siting the Blacker Bombards, later to be known as spigot mortars. The Mobile Column obtained three 6-pounder guns and formed an artillery troop under Capt. J. S. Woolley, M.C., an ex-gunner with a fine record in the Great War.

Facilities for central training were increased. The S.P.A. Home Guard School at Bulford was highly successful. Nearly 200 officers and men attended the junior leaders' course, whilst 34 qualified and received certificates as grenade instructors.

In the autumn the first battle drill instruction arrived and the Adjutant's

Demonstration Squad was formed from members of the Avon Valley Platoon. This squad gave a demonstration to the Battalion, which was attended by many staff officers from S.P.A. As a result the Area Commander ordered that it should be repeated in front of representatives from all the Home Guard battalions in Wiltshire.

The Battalion shooting competition was won by Wilton Platoon. On 22nd November, Sgt. J. Williamson, of Alderbury Company, obtained an " A " at Woolacombe. This was the first " A " to be won by a Wiltshire Home Guard. Week-end T.E.W.T.S. for officers and senior N.C.O.s were held in the winter, and N.C.O.'s refresher courses were instituted by Battalion H.Q. as a preliminary to cadre classes in 1943.

" George Cross " for Gallantry

On 13th, September Lt. W. Foster, M.C., D.C.M., of Alderbury Company, lost his life whilst supervising the throwing of No. 36 grenades by members of an A.A. battery. He deliberately laid himself on a grenade which had rolled back into the throwing position at the feet of the thrower. Lt. Foster's great gallantry was officially recognised and on 27th November it was announced by the B.B.C. that he had received the posthumous award of the George Cross.

On 1st January 1943, Lt.-Col. Phillips received further extension of service. Maj. Cameron resigned as Second in Command, and the position was not filled. Capt. F. F. McNeil was appointed Battalion Intelligence Officer with the rank of lieutenant with effect from 1st January 1943. On 5th April, C.S.M. Dench was appointed a second P.S.I.

Two companies were sub-divided. In March the Downton Company was placed under Maj. C. C. Parson, and Ebble Valley Company under Maj. Lord Essex, and in September Amesbury Company, comprising Amesbury and Avon Valley, was formed under Maj. Faris, O.B.E., whilst Cholderton and Winterbourne Gunner became Cholderton Company, under Maj. L. Edmunds. Bourne Valley Company, having shed Winterbourne Gunner, became composed of C.D.E.S. personnel only. The Mobile Column were issued with ten armoured recce. cars and on its first appearance in the city the detachment received a great ovation. These cars were a very welcome addition as hitherto the " recce " duties had depended on despatch riders, riding their own motor-cycles and without any kind of individual protection.

The operational rôle remained as before but with the emphasis ever stronger on mobility. New weapons arrived in the shape of Boys anti-tank rifles and 2 pounder guns. Great attention was paid to inter-communication within the Battalion. Ample practice ammunition of all calibre was issued and many local ranges were authorised.

Three more " A " Certificates were obtained at Woolacombe : Sgt. Howden, Bourne Valley Company, on 30th May, 1943 ; Corp. M. Bowers, Bourne Valley Company, on 30th May 1943 ; and Corp. H. J. Burrows, Amesbury Company, on 22nd August 1943. The Battalion shooting competition was won by Bourne Valley Company.

The Third Anniversary

On 16th May the Battalion joined with the 8th Battalion in a ceremonial parade, culminating in a march past at the saluting base in the Market Square Salisbury, where the G.O.C.-in-C. Southern Command, Gen. H. C. Loyd, took the salute. The Battalion fell in with its head at the Chipper Lane exit to Castle Street, and stretched back via Endless Street and Albany Road to Wyndham Road. All companies sent large contingents, the total strength of the Battalion in the parade being about 1,400.

The Battalion had the good fortune to be nominated to provide one other rank to represent the County of Wiltshire Home Guard at an armed parade and march past of the Home Guard in Central London. The honour was given to Sgt. A. Howden, of Bourne Valley Company, who carried out the duty in an exemplary manner.

During the summer successful week-end camps were held at Lyburn House on the borders of the New Forest. The first camp was opened on 22nd May by Col. Fleming, the Sub-Area Commander, and camps continued until 10th October ,when they ceased only because Bolero took over the house. The assault course and battalion inoculation practice were both run as tests of leadership, and names of those who did well were published in orders. In this way many first class N.C.O.s were discovered. The camp was allocated to all companies in the Battalion and many of them paid two and even three visits. Attendances were always up to capacity. Many distinguished officers visited the camp and expressed admiration for the efficiency of the instruction, the excellence of the organisation and the enthusiasm of the students.

During the winter of 1943–44, 610 officers and other ranks qualified under the new proficiency tests as laid down in the War Office booklet dated 19th May 1943, and a further 11 officers and N.C.O.s were tested by the Adjutant and P.S.I.s and received Battalion H.Q.s Certificates as qualified grenade instructors.

On 1st November Lt.-Col. A. E. Phillips was replaced, under the over-age rule, as Battalion Commander by Maj.-Gen. Geoffrey Brooke, who handed over command of the Mobile Column to Maj. J. C. Wyatt, at that time the column Adjutant. Lt.-Col. Rupert Stephens became Battalion Second in Command. At the end of 1943 the Battalion consisted of ten companies and an M.T. company, with a total strength of 2,433. The organisation of " F " Company, the Mobile Column, was : H.Q. staff S. and I. and Mobile Ambulances ; H.Q. Squadron, one troop anti-tank guns (2-pounder and 6-pounder), three troops armoured recce. cars ; " A " Squadron, three troops (rifles and automatics) ; " B " Squadron, three troops (rifles and automatics).

The importance of this column was considered to be ever increasing and its scope was enlarged to cover the whole Battalion area. To compete with these requirements the column was extended to include Bodenham, Odstock, Whiteparish and Durrington Platoons, the total strength becoming over 350.

Early in the year 1944 the following Battalion H.Q. appointments were made : Lt.-Col. M. W. Emly, O.B.E., T.D., to be Battalion Signals Officer (Lt.), Lt. G. W.

Bourne to be Battalion Press Officer (Lt.), Capt. J. S. Woolley, M.C., to be Battalion Artillery Training Officer (Lt.). In July Lt. Emly resigned and Lt. W. W. King became Battalion Signals Officer. Owing to pressure of civilian work Maj. Parsons relinquished the command of the Downton Company, which was taken over by Maj. E. T. M. Moody.

Operational Guards

In the spring and early summer a number of operational guards were found. Mobile Column and Larkhill Platoon found guards at Hampshire and Dorset District Headquarters and Southern Sector Headquarters respectively, whilst Downton, Alderbury, Bourne Valley and Cholderton Companies found railway guards. In common with other Home Guard battalions the men who formed these guards have received the thanks of the Com.-in-Chf. Home Forces, and there is no doubt that the Home Guard made a real contribution to the successful invasion of the Continent.

Training after the stand down of the guards was greatly relaxed, the emphasis being now placed on basic weapon training.

A camp took place at Fovant, where the main items were night firing and a battle attack with live ammunition and grenades. It says much for the spirit of the Battalion that the camp ran from the first week-end in June to the last week-end in August. The Battalion shooting competition was won by a team from Winterbourne Gunner Platoon, representing Cholderton Company.

Since the inception of the Local Defence Volunteers, 676 members of the 7th Battalion left to join His Majesty's Forces, and yet the total strength of the Battalion never fell below its " ceiling ".

On 3rd December a ceremonial parade of the 7th and 8th Battalions took place in Salisbury. The Battalion assembled at the Council House, marched through the city and past the G.O.C.-in-C. Southern Command, and returned to the Council House for a farewell speech by the Commanding Officer and a final march past. In spite of the distances involved, nearly 1,200 men paraded, and everything went, as always with the 7th, with clock-like precision. The men marched with great spirit and fine drill, proud of themselves and of the part they had played. In his farewell speech Gen. Brooke recalled the circumstances that had led to the formation of the Battalion, congratulated the men on their keenness and good work, and hoped that the spirit and comradeship of the Home Guard would never die out.

It is clear that his words fell on fruitful ground because already companies are forming old comrades' associations and affiliating with the Battalion Old Comrades' Association, which has Gen. Brooke as President, Capt. C. J. Lee as Hon. Secretary and Lt. Norman H. Austin as Treasurer. Eleven rifle clubs are being formed.

One hundred and thirty-five women were enrolled as members of the Battalion and their help in the orderly rooms, at feeding centres and in other directions was greatly appreciated. They were known as Women Home Guard Auxiliaries.

On 21st December it became known that Maj. J. C. Wyatt had been awarded the M.B.E. and Sgt. Wallis the B.E.M. for their fine work in the Home Guard, and on this fitting note this short account of the Battalion can rightly be closed.

8TH BATTALION WILTSHIRE HOME GUARD

NOTES ON FORMATION AND GROWTH OF UNIT

1. As a result of the broadcast appeal on 14th May 1940, the Salisbury City Police during the days that followed were, like the Police throughout the country, inundated with applications to join the Local Defence Volunteers. So great was the urgency of the times that within a week zones and sub-areas had been formed, and the Police applications were being dealt with, in Salisbury, by Maj.-Gen. G. H. B. Freeth, C.B., C.M.G., D.S.O. with a view to the formation of a company of the Local Defence Volunteers in the city.

2. Thus about the middle of May 1940 the " Sarum City Company " came into being, and in due course became No. 5 Company of the Salisbury Battalion, Local Defence Volunteers (the late Maj.-Gen. W. P. H. Hill, C.B., C.M.G., D.S.O. commanding).

The Company comprised three platoons and some factory defence units as follows :

Company Commander	Maj.-Gen. G. H. B. Freeth, C.B., C.M.G., D.S.O.
Secretary and Assistant	Mr. G. S. Fawcett
No. 14 Platoon Commander	Maj.-Gen. Sir H. de C. Martelli, K.B.E., D.S.O.
Assistants	1. Mr. H. G. Sainsbury, then Mr. G. Nichols, 2. Mr. L. H. Belben, 3. Mr. Gunstone, then Mr. H. Bannell, 4. Capt. C. H. Latimer Needham
No. 15 Platoon Commander	Brig. H. J. G. Gale, D.S.O.
Assistants	1. Capt. W. H. R. Blacking, 2. Maj. J. A. Radford, M.C., 3. Mr. C. H. Robinson
No. 16 Platoon Commander	Lt.-Col. F. W. Vanderkiste, D.S.O.
Assistants	1. Capt. H. Bailey, M.C., 2. Mr. T. Elliott, 3. Mr. L. A. Sly

Company Headquarters were at first at 56 The Close (Gen. Freeth) and later at 89 Crane Street. Platoon headquarters were situated as follows :

No. 14 Platoon   Gunstone's Offices and St. Thomas School
No. 15   ,,   21 The Close (Capt. Blacking)
No. 16   ,,   White Hart Garage

At the Crane Street Headquarters, the clerical work, by no means inconsiderable, was carried out in an honorary capacity by Mr. F. J. Moore (now Lt.) and by Mrs. D. M. Finn—both still with the unit.

3. In June 1940 the average strength of the platoons was 200. Sub-units, afterwards attached to the platoons, were formed for factory defence ; these were :

Wiltshire and Dorset Bus Company Mr. H. J. Crabbe
Salisbury Electric Light Company Mr. W. J. Deacon (now Maj. A. C. F.)
Salisbury Gas Company Mr. Downer
Nestles Milk Factory Mr. A. W. Crick
R.A.F. L.D.V. Platoon, Old Sarum Mr. H. C. Egerton

4. On 1st October 1940 the Sarum City Company was formed into a battalion known as the " 8th (Sarum City) Battalion Wiltshire Home Guard ", and the following appointments were made :

Battalion Commander	Maj.-Gen. G. H. B. Freeth, C.B., C.M.G., D.S.O. (BC)
Battalion Second in Command	Maj.-Gen. Sir H. de C. Martelli, K.B.E., C.B., D.S.O. (CC)
Officer i/c Training	Brig. H. J. Gale, D.S.O. (CC)
Adjutant	Capt. W. H. R. Blacking (CC)
Quartermaster	Mr. C. H. Robinson (PC)
Transport Officer	Mr. A. M. O'Brien (PC)
Battalion Works Officer	Lt.-Col. D. H. Keelan, V.D. (PC)
H.Q. Company Commander	Lt.-Col. F. W. Vanderkiste, D.S.O. (CC)
" A " (No. 1) Company	Mr. G. S. Fawcett (CC)
" B " (No. 2) Company	Maj. J. A. Radford, M.C. (CC)
" C " (No. 3) Company	Mr. C. B. Gibbs (CC)

(BC)—Volunteer rank of Battalion Commander (A.C.I. 924/40 para. 6)
(CC)—   ,,   ,,   ,, Company Commander
(PC)—   ,,   ,,   ,, Platoon Commander

Battalion Headquarters were at this time situated in Bridge Street (two rooms)' and the Quartermasters Stores in a large loft in Crane Street (Crown Hotel).

The first Battalion Order was published on 4th October 1940, and Parts 1 and 11 Battalion Orders have been published without break on Wednesday every week from that date until the present time.

5. On the 1st Feb. 1941 the Battalion entered a new phase, and with effect from that date Home Guard commissions were given to the foregoing officers and to others in the unit. Although no definite establishment was laid down, each battalion set about organising itself on the lines of a Regular military establishment. In the 8th Battalion the appointment of personnel for Battalion Headquarters and companies was now carried out on the basis of an infantry battalion.

The Headquarters of the Battalion were now situated at 27 Fisherton Street, and the Quartermasters Stores, hitherto in the Crane Street loft, were moved to more convenient quarters in the stables of Mompesson House, The Close. The Quartermaster was assisted by Mr. (now Lt.) S. J. Smith as R.Q.M.S.

At this time the strength of the Battalion was over 700. All were fully clothed with battle dress and boots although complete equipment had not been issued. At the end of the previous December, the Battalion had exchanged ·303 rifles for ·300 rifles, of which the unit held 610.

In May 1941 Lt.-Col. G. H. B. Freeth was appointed the first Group Commander (South Wiltshire), and Maj. Sir H. de C. Martelli succeeded him as Battalion Commander in the rank of Lt.-Col. The appointment of Battalion Second in Command remained in abeyance for the time being.

On 1st October 1941 Col. W. Elliott, C.B., C.B.E., D.S.O., who had been transferred from the 7th Battalion Wiltshire Home Guard, was appointed Battalion Second in Command in the rank of major.

6. Members of the old Local Defence Volunteer unit viewed the issue of the " Conscription " Act (151 of 1942) with not a little disquiet, but few took advantage of the clause that allowed resignation from the force up to the 16th February 1942. An increase in ceilings for operational purposes was at that time essential, and on the whole officers and other ranks loyally recognised the need. The outcome of conscription in the 8th Battalion was an increase in strength from 645 in the early spring of 1942 to 1,170 in January 1943. In the meantime, calling up age limits were on the increase. On 3rd June 1942 a new company, " D " Company was formed from the " Factory " Platoon provided by the Wiltshire and Dorset Bus Company under command of Capt. (now Maj.) G. R. E. Wallis. One platoon of the new company undertook the maintenance of the Battalion transport.

By July 1943 there were 34 nominated Women Auxiliaries.

7. Permanent Staff. In December of 1940 Mr. H. Northover, an original " platoon " commander of Local Defence Volunteer days, was enlisted in the Army and was appointed P.S.I. to the Battalion, an appointment which he held until October 1943.

In July 1942 Capt. C. R. M. Hutchinson, Durham Light Infantry, was posted as Adjutant and took over training and operational duties ; and in the following month Capt. W. H. R. Blacking, who resigned his Home Guard commission for the purpose, received a commission in the Army and was appointed Captain for A. & Q. Duties to deal with the administration of the Battalion.

At the present time there are three P.S.I.s—Sgts. Lodwick and Voss for assistance in training, and Sgt. Flint for assistance in administration.

8. In July 1942 Lt.-Col. Sir H. de C. Martelli retired on reaching the age limit in the Home Guard, and Maj. W. Elliott was appointed to command the Battalion in the rank of Lt.-Col.

Consequent on the withdrawal of infantry reinforcements from Salisbury Tank Island defences, a new company, " F " Company, was formed in November of this year (1942) with Capt. (now Maj.) L. A. Sly in command ; and on the 1st December the original " B " Company was divided into two smaller companies, viz. " B " Company under command of Maj. S. Collett and " E " Company under command of Capt. (now Maj.) G. J. Venman. Later, Maj. Collett was appointed Battalion Second in Command, and the command of " B " Company passed to Capt. (now Maj.) S. Leaman.

94

The original H.Q. Company, which had consisted of Battalion Headquarter details and of certain " factory " units, was reorganised in August 1943 ; Battalion Headquarter personnel were formed into a platoon (No. 25) which included Signals, Intelligence and Administrative Sections—the latter absorbing the existing Supplies Section—under the command of Lt. J. R. Morgan, M.M., and the remainder of the old H.Q. Company became " H " Company.

9. At the present time, September 1944, companies of the 8th Battalion are commanded as follows :

" A " Company :
    Maj. D. McWilliam, M.C.
" B " Company : Maj. S. Leaman
" C " Company : Maj. C. B. Gibbs
" D " Company : Maj. G. R. E. Wallis

" E " Company : Maj. G. J. Venman
" F " Company : Maj. L. A. Sly
" H " Company : Maj. G. M. Warry
26 *Platoon* (*R.A.F. Old Sarum*) :
    Lt. C. A. Payne

In addition to the Battalion Commander and his Second in Command and permanent staff, there are at Battalion Headquarters :

Medical Officer : Maj. F. L. Buttar
W/Trg. Officer : Capt. W. Radford
Accounts : Lt. F. J. Moore
Ammunition Officer : Lt. R. Collins
Civil Defence Liaison :
    Capt. R. J. C. Maunsell, O.B.E.
Chief Guide : Lt. W. A. Page
Gas Officer : Lt. A. S. G. Hill
25 *Platoon Commander* :
    Lt. J. R. Morgan, M.M.
Quartermaster :
    Capt. C. H. Robinson, M.B.E.

Musketry : Lt. H. D. M. Lywood
Messing Officer : Lt. S. J. Smith
M.L.O. and Press :
    Lt. J. H. R. Bennett
Intelligence Officer :
    Lt. H. Bailey, M.C.
Signals Officer :
    Lt. W. E. C. Broadway
Sector L.O. : Lt. C. T. Cusworth
Typists : Mrs. D. M. Finn and Miss K. Parken
Women Auxiliaries : Mrs. S. Collett

From September 1943 the Headquarters of the Battalion have been situated at the Wiltshire Territorial Army Association Drill Hall, Salisbury.

10. Of the many activities and duties carried out by the Battalion since its inception the following may be mentioned :

Manning observation posts in the country around Salisbury ;
Manning check-points (examination of identity cards, etc.) in 1940 ;
Factory guards ;
Fireguard duties at Salisbury Cathedral and Salisbury Infirmary ;
Fireguard street pickets ;
V.P. guard duties and patrols (1944).

Upwards of 350 members of the Battalion have joined His Majesty's Forces since its formation in 1940.

Up to September 1944, one M.B.E. and eight Certificates of Good Service have been awarded to members of the Battalion.

From the beginning, the Battalion has been keenly interested in the Army Cadet movement, and it may be regarded as the." parent " of the 8th Battalion (Salisbury City) Wiltshire Army Cadet Force, commanded by Maj. W. J. Deacon, one of the original Home Guard officers in the Battalion.

W. H. R. BLACKING, Capt.

for Lt.-Col. Commanding.

9TH BATTALION WILTSHIRE HOME GUARD

Formation and Organisation

IMMEDIATELY after Mr. Eden's broadcast, men from all walks of life came forward to volunteer, and to give in their names to the local Police.

In the meantime Gen. the Hon. Sir F. Gathorne Hardy, G.C.B., G.C.V.O., D.S.O., who had recently relinquished the Aldershot Command, and come to live in Wiltshire, was instructed by the War Office to organise the Force in the county.

On 18th May he 'phoned Brig.-Gen. H. F. E. Lewin, C.B., C.M.G., and asked him if he would raise a battalion in North Wiltshire, and, if so, would he come to a conference at Lockeridge on 19th May.

At this conference it was decided that Gen. Lewin should form the 9th Battalion within the Highworth Rural District and the Cricklade and Wootton Bassett Rural District, the Borough of Swindon being left for the 5th Battalion.

Gen. Lewin's first step was to contact all local Police to get names of likely persons in the parishes who would help, and ask them to come to a conference at Salthrop House on 20th May. The following attended this conference :

Maj. F. W. Barrett from Wroughton
Mr. A. D. Passmore from Wanborough
Mr. J. M. Farrant from Wootton Bassett
Maj. B. Van de Weyer from South Marston
Capt. H. R. Ward from Purton
Capt. S. Dennis from Cricklade
Mr. J. M. Mordaunt from Ashton Keynes

These gentlemen were given the task of raising detachments in their own, and, in some cases, their neighbouring parishes. The general procedure adopted was to call parish and village meetings. These were usually crowded with men from all walks of life, young and old. Volunteers were enrolled between the ages of 17 and 75, and within a few days the Battalion was 1,000 strong, being made up of the following six companies, with Battalion Headquarters at Salthrop House, Wroughton :

Cricklade Company.—Commanded by Captain Dennis, with platoons at Cricklade, Ashton Keynes, Leigh, Latton, Marston Meysey and Eisey.

Highworth Company.—Commanded by Maj. Van de Weyer, with platoons at Highworth, South Marston, Stratton, Hannington and Castle Eaton.

Wanborough Company.—Commanded by Mr. Passmore, with platoons at Wanborough, Liddington, Bishopstone, Hinton and Foxhill.

Wroughton Company.—Commanded by Maj. Barrett, with platoons at Salthrop, Wroughton, Overtown, Wroughton Airfield, Elcombe and Chiseldon.

Wootton Bassett Company.—Commanded by Mr. Farrant, with platoons at Wootton Bassett, Lyneham, Tockenham, Broad Town, Bushton and Clyffe Pypard.

Purton Company.—Commanded by Capt. Ward, with platoons at Purton, Braydon, Blunsdon, Lydiard Millicent, Lydiard Tregoze and Purton Stoke.

Company commanders split their companies, and formed platoons in villages and hamlets where the numbers of volunteers warranted them, and each commander usually nominated his platoon commanders. Sections again were formed according to locality, but, as a rule, sections elected their own section leaders. It was only natural, and no doubt wise at the time, that old soldiers found themselves as leaders.

It was very fortunate that no fixed establishments were laid down. This enabled units and detachments to be formed where expedient, and would have facilitated expeditious mustering had an emergency arisen.

Thus when, at the end of June, it was found that some companies as first formed were too unwieldy, reorganisation took place. Chiseldon was lopped off Wroughton Company, and was formed into a company under the command of Mr. N. L. Whatley, with platoons at Hodson, Chiseldon, Badbury and Coate.

Blunsdon was detached from Purton Company, and put under the command of Lt.-Col. Parsons, with platoons at Blunsdon, Castle Eaton and Hannington.

Ashton Keynes was turned into a company under the command of Mr. J. M. Mordaunt.

Also about this time, Capt. Maurice Kingscote took over the Wanborough Company from Mr. Passmore, who resigned, and Col. A. Canning, C.M.G., took over the Purton Company, as he was more in the centre of the Company area than Capt. Ward. The latter became Second in Command, and also Praydon Platoon Commander.

The organising of the Battalion up to this stage had been accomplished by Gen. Lewin with practically no staff. It was some weeks before he was able to secure the services of a Great War associate, Capt. Pidgeon, as Adjutant Quartermaster and general factotum.

The fact that the Battalion Headquarters was situated at Salthrop, a small and scattered hamlet situated right on the edge of the Battalion area, did not facilitate matters, and precluded the use of the Local Defence Volunteers for Headquarters staff work.

A Battalion conference was held weekly in Swindon—at first, by kind permission of Mr. J. M. Farrant, at his offices, and later at the Railway Hotel in Newport Street. These conferences continued weekly up to 28th December 1944, and most company commanders, or their second in commands, attended regularly.

The Battalion continued as thus constituted until companies were formed at airfields situated in the Battalion area—viz., Wroughton—April 1941 ; Lyneham—July 1941 ; Clyffe Pypard—November 1941, and, in 1943, a second company at the Wroughton Airfield, with a platoon at Marine Mountings Factory at North Wroughton.

In January 1943, the Lower Stratton Platoon was transferred to the 220 (101 Wiltshire Home Guard) " Z " A.A. Battery, and in May 1943 the Upper Stratton Platoon were taken from the Highworth Company and put into the newly-formed 11th Factory Battalion.

Up to March 1941 unit and sub-unit commanders were designated as battalion commander, company commander, platoon leader and section leader. But then rankings as in the Regular Army were initiated as follows :

Battalion Commander	Lieutenant-Colonel
Battalion Second in Command	Major
Company Commander	Major or Captain
Company Second in Command	Captain or Lieutenant
Platoon Commander	Lieutenant or Second Lieutenant

with appropriate C.S.M., C.Q.M.S., sergeants, corporals and lance-corporals.

In June 1941, Capt. Pidgeon was killed in an accident in London, and it was July 1941, before his successor, Capt. E. H. Robinson, K.R.R.C., was appointed. He was recalled to his unit early in August, and Capt. J. O. Naismith, D.S.O., took over Adjutant's duties on 22nd August 1941, an appointment he retained until Capt. E. J. Hawxwell, of the K.R.R.C., was appointed Adjutant and Training Officer for the Battalion early in March 1942.

Capt. Naismith was then appointed Battalion Quartermaster, and remained with the Battalion as such until the " bitter end ".

Compulsory service came into force in February 1942, and the Battalion lost less than 100 men due to resignations. These were made up subsequently by directed enrolments, the first of whom came in August 1942.

In July 1941, a P.S.I. was added to Battalion Establishment, and Sgt. Sims, of the Wiltshire Regiment, was seconded to the 9th Battalion. Another P.S.I. was added in September 1942, and Sgt. Dye, of the K.R.R.C. joined the Battalion, and both were given the temporary rank of C.S.M.

Battalion permanent staff establishments were also extended to include civilian storemen and clerks, and in November 1941, companies were also allowed to engage whole or part time storemen-clerks. These could be Home Guards or otherwise.

In January 1942, Army Council instructions were issued to the effect that all Home Guards over 65—except in very exceptional cases—should resign or be discharged. This caused much heart-burning at the time, and necessitated the reorganising of several commands.

Lt.-Col. Lewin, who had organised the Battalion with practically no staff, and had done all the spade work, had perforce to resign, very much against his wishes. His Second in Command, Col. Parsons, took over the command of the Battalion, and Capt. Howard took over the Blunsdon Company. Battalion Headquarters was moved to the King and Queen Hotel, Highworth, on 16th February 1942.

Battalion Headquarters was now in a position to direct, organise and help companies with their training in the use of the more complicated and heavier arms and equipment that had now been issued.

The following officers also had to resign :

31 March 1942.—Major B. Van de Weyer handed Highworth Company over over to Capt. F. W. Jennings.

31 March 1942.—Maj. A. Canning handed Purton Company over to Capt. R. H. Ward.

31 Dec. 1942.—Maj. F. W. Barrett handed Wroughton Company over to Capt. W. Gosling, V.C.

31 Dec. 1942.—Maj. S. Dennis handed Cricklade Company over to Capt. R. W. Cainey.

1 Sept. 1942.—Capt. R. H. Ward handed Purton Company over to Capt. W. E. Orsborn.

In March 1942, Maj. M. Kingscote, on leaving the district, relinquished his command of the Wanborough Company to Capt. R. H. Wilson, M.C. In July 1944, Maj. F. W. Jennings and Capt. S. A. Bonner, O.B.E., left the district, whereupon Sir Noel Arkell took over the Highworth Company. Maj. Jennings had been nominated Second in Command of the Battalion, and now Maj. N. L. Whatley, Officer Commanding Chiseldon Company, was appointed and handed the Chiseldon Company over to his Second in Command, Capt. E. Hughes, M.M. The Battalion ceiling was set at 2,320. The highest strength reached was 2,340, and never fell below 2,100, and upon " Stand down " the Battalion strength was 96 officers and 2,028 other ranks, and the various headquarters were made up as follows :

Battalion Headquarters

Commanding Officer : Lt.-Col. A. W. Parsons, C.M.G., D.S.O.
Second in Command :
Maj. N. L. Whatley
Adjutant :
Capt. E. J. Hawxwell, K.R.R.C.
Quartermaster :
Capt. J. O. Naismith, M.A., D.S.O.
Permant Staff Instructors : C.S.M. E. E. Sims, Wilts. Regt., C.S.M. E. Dye, K.R.R.C.

" A " Company

Company Headquarters :
Ashton Keynes
Company Commander :
Maj. J. M. Mordaunt
Second in Command :
Lt. W. G. Wilkins

" B " Company

Company Headquarters : Cricklade
Company Commander :
Maj. R. W. Cainey
Second in Command :
Capt. W. M. Carter
C.S.M. : W. S. Newman
C.Q.M.S. : E. O. Hammond
Platoon Commanders : Lt. N. F. J. Wilkins, Sgt. E. G. Richens, Lt. H. T. Carter, Sgt. E. F. Carpenter, Lt. C. Horton, Sgt. P. Giles, Lt. A. R. Lee, Sgt. J. H. Curtis, Lt. S. L. Maundrell, Sgt. W. G. Fiddler.

" C " Company

Company Headquarters : Blundson
Company Commander :
Maj. J. A. G. Howard
Second in Command :
Capt. K. H. Tucker

"C" COMPANY (Continued)

C.S.M. : K. W. Deacon
C.Q.M.S. : G. Brown
Platoon Commanders : Lt. B. Hoddinott Sgt. N. G. Coxhead, 2/Lt. C. R. O. Ayres, Sgt. C. A. Warr, Lt. T. Green, Sgt. E. G. Adams, Lt. S. W. Maundrell, Sgt. E. A. V. Adams, 2/Lt. E. Ward Sgt. W. T. Stretten.

"D" Company

Company Headquarters : Highworth
Company Commander :
Maj. Sir T. Noel Arkell
Second in Command : Capt. L. Cotton
C.S.M. : W. H. Avery
C.Q.M.S. : F. T. Chick
Platoon Commanders : Lt. H. D. Roberts, Sgt. H. Jefferies, Lt. L. C. Hicks, Sgt. T. Slack, Lt. C. C. Morse, Sgt. J. J. Cook, 2/Lt. E. F. Fry, Sgt. G. H. Hemmings, Lt. G. Miles, M.M., Sgt. A. Fry.

"E" Company

Company Headquarters : Wanborough
Company Commander :
Maj. R. H. Wilson, M.C.
Second in Command :
Capt. E. A. Merricks
C.S.M. : J. Fisher
C.Q.M.S. : E. B. L. Colborne
Platoon Commanders : Lt. R. B. Henderson, Sgt. R. Culverwell, Lt. E. W. Roberts, Sgt. S. E. Lewis, P.S.M. W. J. Pound, Sgt. R. Archer, Lt. E. W. Kitchen, Sgt. F. R. Kent, Lt. F. Carter, Sgt. S. A. Nash.

"F" Company

Company Headquarters : Badbury
Company Commander :
Maj. E. A. Hughes, M.M.

Second in Command :
Capt. D. E. Huck
C.S.M. : P. E. Snook
C.Q.M.S. : W. S. Perry
Platoon Commanders : Lt. C. N. Whatlay, Sgt. G. E. Jones, Lt. F. Akehurst, Sgt. A. Bryant, 2/Lt. T. Ford, Sgt. A. S. Reeves, 2/Lt. K. Dale, Sgt. J. B. Wilmer.

"G" Company

Company Headquarters : Wroughton
Company Commander :
Maj. W. Gosling, V.C.
Second in Command :
Capt. O. Thomas
C.S.M. : H. C. Pickett
C.Q.M.S. : C. E. Hacker
Platoon Commanders : Lt. J. A. T. Page, Sgt. C. Hawkins, Lt. C. E. Rowden, Sgt. J. Cole, Lt. W. G. Prismall, M.M., Sgt. C. J. Ody, Lt. A. F. Brain, Sgt. W. J. Hatherall, Lt. S. V. Griffin, Sgt. A. H. Pinnell, Lt. T. C. Curtis, Sgt. F. E. Barrett, Lt. F. T. White, Sgt. A. W. Llewellyn

"H" Company

Company Headquarters :
Wootton Bassett
Company Commander :
Maj. J. M. Farrant, M.B.E.
Second in Command :
Capt. W. B. V. Clarke
C.S.M. : A. J. Walker
C.Q.M.S. : E. A. Westcott
Platoon Commanders : 2/Lt. J. E. Mapson, Sgt. H. G. A. Compton, Lt. F. W. Stratton, Sgt. L. S. D. Dixon, Lt. C. G. Collett, Sgt. R. J. P. Cooksay, Lt. W. M. Burbidge, Sgt. C. Gough, Lt. R. J. Mifln, Sgt. S. I. Stickler, Lt. R. C. Hicks, Sgt. A. E. Pickett.

" I " Company

Company Headquarters : Purton
Company Commander :
Maj. W. E. Orsborn
Second in Command :
Capt. H. A. Webber
C.S.M. : W. E. Biggs
C.Q.M.S. : L. F. Barnes
Platoon Commanders : 2/Lt. P. R. Painter, Sgt. W. Paish, Lt. F. G. Neville, M.M., Sgt. T. C. Grant, 2/Lt. G. R. Gantlett, Sgt. A. T. Waldron, Lt. A. Druett, Sgt. B. H. Dash, Lt. H. B. Mills, Sgt. E. King, 2/Lt. F. J. Shailes, Sgt. L. H. Johnson

" J " Company

Company Headquarters :
R.A.F. Wroughton. No. 26 M.U.
Company Commander :
Capt. E. A. Preece, M.M.
Second in Command :
Lt. A. G. Smith
C.Q.M.S. : A. L. Fox
Platoon Commanders : 2/Lt. H. Jones, Sgt. A. C. Barlow, 2/Lt. E. G. Coe, Sgt. G. R. Grievson.

" K " Company

Company Headquarters :
R.A.F. Wroughton. No. 15 M.U.
Company Commander :
Capt. W. Middleton, B.E.M.
Second in Command : Lt. W. Langley
C.S.M. : A. W. Richards
C.Q.M.S. : W. Dawe
Platoon Commanders : Lt. T. A. Mason, Sgt. S. F. Embling, 2/Lt. W. T. Blackman, Sgt. C. T. Fisher, Lt. H. Jarman, Sgt. W. C. Longcroft, Lt. F. Shaw, Sgt. C. Acaster, 2/Lt. E. E. Spicer, Sgt. G. Evans.

" L " Company

Company Headquarters : R.A.F. Clyffe Pypard. No. 29 E.F.T.S.
Company Commander :
Capt. B. Browne
Second in Command : Lt. C. T. Hall
C.Q.M.S. : E. E. McHale
Platoon Commanders : 2/Lt. R. Goodson, Sgt. A. Horswell, 2/Lt. J. C. Catesby, Sgt. K. L. Hayward, Sgt. A. E. Snowden.

" M " Company

Company Headquarters :
R.A.F. Lyneham. No. 33 M.U.
Company Commander :
Capt. H. D. Shipp
Second in Command :
Lt. H. V. Dexter
C.S.M. : W. H. M. Rogers
C.Q.M.S. : R. W. Wright
Platoon Commanders : 2/Lt. W. G. Clark, Sgt. A. E. Brown, 2/Lt. S. A. Denney, Corp. R. H. Naylor, 2/Lt. A. G. Clark, Sgt. S. J. Jarvis, Lt. A. H. Harrison, Sgt. C. Simms.

At various dates the following additional appointments were made to the Battalion Headquarters :
Ammunition Officer :
Lt. B. Van de Weyer
Medical Officer : Maj. J. M. Davidson
Battalion Accountant :
Lt. B. L. Monahan
Signalling Officers : Lt. K. F. Hall, 2/Lt. V. J. Webb
Transport Officer : Lt. H. M. Dixon
Liaison Officer : Lt. H. E. V. Pryor
Intelligence Officer :
2/Lt. J. E. Douglas

Operational Role

This was not agreed upon for some months, and at the time caused considerable anxiety and delay in appropriate training. Now, looking back, this is understandable, for one can visualise the springing up, overnight almost, of a force one and threequarter millions strong, with no arms available, and yet with the enemy metaphorically at our doors, and literally liable to be dropped at them.

The first danger appeared to be from Fifth Columnists, for on 31st May 1940, road-blocks were erected on all main roads throughout the country, and all traffic stopped and checked from an hour before sunset to an hour after dawn.

This went on for some weeks. Then numbers of road-blocks were reduced, and eventually removed entirely, but not before there had been some " incidents " —fortunately none serious.

One evening about dusk, the Police 'phoned up one company reporting that suspicious characters had been seen in a car moving towards the Company area. Patrols that had moved off were contacted. A car appeared from the direction indicated, and failed to stop when challenged, but soon changed its mind when one round was fired at the back wheel, and ricochetted under the driver's seat. This car did not fail to stop when challenged by another patrol from the same company.

Railways were being patrolled, and vulnerable points guarded for the same periods.

Eventually it was laid down that the rôle of the 9th Battalion was to deny the enemy free passage through the Battalion area.

For this purpose Highworth, Cricklade and Wootton Bassett, being centres of communication, were designated centres of resistance, through which no enemy was to be allowed to pass.

The rural companies were to get information and report, destroy the enemy if possible, but, at any cost, delay and harrass them.

The airfield companies were concerned with the defence of their airfields, and local rural units co-operated with them.

Home Guards, of course, were expected to help the Civil Defence when and where they could. Liaison with them was carried out by a Home Guard representative being a member of Local and District Invasion Committees.

Home Guards were entrusted with the immobilisation of petrol pumps in their areas should the necessity arise.

Clothing and Equipment

Because of its dispersal over an area of some 150 square miles, the clothing and equipping of the 9th Battalion was of necessity a slow and tedious performance. Supplies came through in dribs and drabs to Battalion Headquarters, from whence there was no transport available for distribution to companies.

Some companies also had little or no transport, and, where they had private cars or lorries available, few had time to fetch the stuff.

103

For some weeks the only distinguishing marks of the Force were the " L.D.V." armlets, and these of course had to be changed for " Home Guard " when the title of the Force was altered.

Khaki denim overalls became available in June, but it was some months before every man was fitted out, and at first they were kept for men going on duty. Field service caps were forthcoming at about the same time, but only in small sizes ! in fact some Home Guards never did get caps large enough for them.

Can it be that in these early days Home Guards were so swollen-headed that the usual Army fittings were too small !

It was understandable in February 1941, when battle dress trousers could not be produced with short enough legs to agree with the waist required. Middle-age spread was to be expected even on war diet !

With men putting in many hours a week patrolling the roads and railway tracks, it is not surprising that the issue of some boots in September was greatly welcomed, but also it was again a long time before men with " extraordinary understandings " could be fitted out.

The colder weather of October increased the clamour for greatcoats, and the winter was over before everyone was supplied. However, some comforts, made or procured by Lady Edwina Lewin, in the shape of gloves, scarves and Balaclava helmets, helped to ease the situation, and he was a rare individual who could not borrow a greatcoat for duty periods.

It was when on night " ops " that this could not be done ! however it has yet to be learned if any Home Guards of this Battalion did succumb to exposure, but at least one case is known where a man on duty at an O.P. *may* have been frozen so stiff that he was unable to return to Headquarters till well after sun-up !

Battle dress began to come through in ones and twos in 1940, but it was February 1941, before any numbers were received, and May before the issue was 100 per cent.

By this time other incidental personal equipment had been coming steadily through, and the Home Guard on its first birthday was more or less fully equipped and proud of it.

When mustering for active operations, Home Guards were expected to bring rations for forty-eight hours. By then it was expected that rations from local sources would be available to start up catering establishments in suitable (or otherwise) premises in platoon areas.

To meet an emergency, ten men packs, or iron rations, were held by companies. These consisted of biscuits, preserved meat, tea, sugar, jam; chocolate and condensed milk.

Through some misunderstanding, some of these were issued, and since they were loosely packed, it is not surprising that when recalled for " turn over " some of the ingredients were not forthcoming ! The replacement issue was packed in sealed tins !

As stated, provision was made for central feeding almost immediately, but it was not until May 1943, that cooking utensils were forthcoming. However, there is no doubt that this difficulty would have been overcome!

Facilities were arranged for the repair of Home Guard boots locally. It cannot be said that the degree of wear and tear was always commensurate with the numbers of parades attended.

Weapons

Sporting guns, a few revolvers and pistols were the only weapons available until June 1941, when a few Canadian Ross ·303 rifles were issued. These never became personal weapons, but were issued to men as they went on duty. They were recalled in July, when considerable numbers of American P.17 ·300 rifles were issued up to about 50 per cent of the Battalion strength. In August this was increased to 80 per cent. These rifles were painted with four-inch red bands near the upper sling swivel, to easily distinguish them from ·303 rifles.

Supply of ·300 S.A.A. was short, and had to be conserved, and therefore very little firing practice was possible with their own rifles for many months. Point 303 rifles were borrowed from units of the Regular Army, and used for firing practice.

" Molotov cocktails " were made, and were the only anti-tank weapons available until the Northover Projector appeared, and was issued one per company in September 1941. Early in October 1940, American ·300 Lewis L.M.G.s with aircraft mountings became available, and were issued one per company, and later increased to approximately three per company.

Twenty-nine m.m. spigot mortars were issued in December 1941, and most companies had two or more with ample 20-pound anti-tank and 14-pound anti-personnel bombs.

A few Smith Guns were held for a few months in 1942, but were soon withdrawn, ostensibly for duty in more vulnerable areas.

Some companies had Browning automatics, and in 1942 all companies received a generous allotment of Sten Guns which enabled every man to have, and hold, a personal weapon. But for a long time insufficient 9 m.m. ammunition was available to enable much firing practice to be carried out. In 1943 issues of ammunition, bombs and grenades, promised to be so heavy that ammunition store-houses were built for every company and platoon in the Battalion.

A few truncheons—rubber—were issued, and would have been useful weapons for night work, but they were recalled when the rubber shortage became acute. They were replaced by truncheons—tubing—in considerable numbers, but, as with the pikes, few ever left Battalion stores.

Issue of Weapons Report

Weapons	Issue Commenced	Completed	Total
Shotguns	May-June 1940	Withdrawn Autumn 1940	
·303 Rifles	June 1940	July 1940	10
·22 ,,			46
·300 ,, A	July 1940	June 1943	1,333
·300 L.M.G.	Oct. 1940	July 1944	34
B.M.G.	Oct. 1941	June 1943	3
T.S.M.G.	April 1941	June 1943	45
B.A.R.s	June 1941	June 1943	8
Northovers	May 1941	Jan. 1942	27
29 Spigot Mortars	Oct. 1941		41
Sten Guns	April 1942	Feb. 1943	514
S.I.P. Grenades	Sept. 1941	May 1942	
36 Grenades	June 1941	July 1944	
68 ,,	Nov. 1941	Dec. 1943	
75 ,,	May 1943	April 1944	
Truncheons, Rubber	Feb. 1941	Withdrawn	70
,, Tubing	Sept. 1941	Sept. 1941	200
Pikes	Aug. 1941	July 1942	
Smith Gun	Sept. 1942	Withdrawn March 1943	6
Vickers	Aug. 1944	Sept. 1944	9
2-Pounder	March 1944		4

Finances

As its original name indicates the Home Guard was unpaid, but its out-of-pocket expenses were largely met in various ways.

Subsistence allowances were granted for expenses incurred for extra food and drink (non-alcoholic) required whilst on duty. In connection with this, extra coupons for tea, sugar and milk were obtainable from the Food Office.

Rents for offices, stores, etc., postage and telephone were chargeable. Mileage claims in respect of the use of motor-cycles, cars, van, lorries and cattle trucks were met. Petrol coupons were issued on a fairly liberal scale, and " G " licences were available for motor-cycles and vehicles which would have been otherwise laid up.

Owners of push-bikes were allowed a halfpenny per mile for maintenance. Buses could also be hired when occasion arose.

In view of the inexpensive nature of the Force, it is regrettable that the authorities showed considerable reluctance in allowing Home Guards to keep their personal clothing. At first it was intended they should keep only their boots. Eventually, after representations from many quarters, Home Guards were allowed to retain their boots, battle dress, greatcoat, cap and gas capes.

TRAINING
General

For a long time, the training of the Home Guard from a battalion point of view must have been a nightmare with no staff and no instructors, except old soldiers from diverse units of the Army which fought in the last war, under vastly different conditions.

To make matters worse, it was some time before the operational rôle of the various companies was established.

In these circumstances it was exceedingly fortunate that in the extreme south of the Battalion area, at Chiseldon Camp, there was stationed the 1st Motor Training Battalion of the K.R.R.C. with a Commanding Officer who was the very essence of help and co-operation.

Nothing was too much trouble for Lt.-Col. E. F. Campbell, D.S.O., and his willing staff of instructors. Arms and equipment were lent for training purposes during the evenings, and on Sundays there were always to be found willing instructors to go with them, in what was their " off time ".

The first essential was to learn to shoot, and for this purpose, and for those who could get there, the miniature range at the camp was nearly always available. Being nearest, Chiseldon, Wanborough and Wroughton Companies were able to make the most of these facilities, but all companies benefited more or less, and especially later, when week-end courses, demonstrations and tactical exercises were arranged.

Some of the other companies had small Army units in their area, and of course benefited from their willing, but necessarily limited, co-operation and help.

Later it was possible to send volunteers for a weeks' training at Home Guard schools, but very few could spare the time, and sometimes it was not always the best men who could get away. However, as a rule, those who did go were of inestimable value upon their return.

But even more beneficial was the Travelling Wing of the Denbies School, which paid its first visit in May 1941, to Cricklade, and later to Chiseldon, Highworth and Blunsdon. They (two or three officers and about six N.C.O.s or other ranks) came prepared to give lectures or demonstrations on topical subjects requested by the Battalion Commanding Officer.

By these means, each company eventually got a nucleus of officers and N.C.O.s capable of giving instruction in most subjects.

Training as a rule was carried out by platoons, particularly in the rural companies, on Sunday mornings from 10.30 to 12.30, and one or two evenings about mid-week from 19.30 to 21.30.

About every three months it was possible for companies to have a Sunday on the open range. In the early days ·303 rifles were borrowed for the day, as ammunition for their own ·300 rifles was not available for practice.

These Sundays were very popular, although it often meant that some missed the only hot midday meal of the week.

The most popular training event was inter-company tactical exercises, but it was usually difficult to obtain sufficient umpires for these, and perhaps that was the reason why higher authorities at one time discouraged them in favour of T.E.W.T.s. The latter, however, were not very popular, and hence were never well attended !

Occasionally practice " action stations " or " stand to " were rehearsed, with usually very gratifying results. Within half an hour of the warning, patrols have been known to be out, and posts manned in skeleton.

Companies usually incorporated some other training with the " turn-out ". For instance, on one occasion, a very rural company was mustered in the very early hours of a Sunday. Patrols were sent out, posts manned and reliefs told off for rest. Then, some time before dawn, milkers were sent home, and the remainder of the company moved off to take up positions preparatory to an attack at dawn on the enemy located in a wood. The signal of the attack was the firing of a 20-pound practice inert bomb from a spigot mortar.

The attack having succeeded, troops moved to a near-by barn for breakfast, and thence to the open range for a shoot for an inter-platoon challenge cup.

It has been known for a prearranged alarm signal not to go off, due to a break in the telephone wire. The only person to arrive at the rendezvous for " battle " was the Battalion Training Officer ! The Company Commander awoke and was terrified, thinking his company must have gone to battle while he overslept !

In October 1941, some ·22 rifles were issued, and most platoons fixed up indoor ranges in skittle alleys, barns or sheds. Lighting was the chief difficulty, but was overcome by the Home Guard initiative and car battery lamps. This enabled shooting practice to be carried out during the winter evenings.

Cloth model landscapes were rigged up and T.E.W.T.s conducted indoors.

When the weather was suitable on winter evenings, inter-platoon tactical exercises were surprisingly popular.

The subjects in which it was most difficult to get men interested were signalling and first aid—the latter particularly.

Bombing and mortar ranges were available as men became proficient enough to make use of them.

The pike was the only weapon that was issued to the Home Guard in which no one took any interest—perhaps because there was no one qualified to give instruction ! There were 100 per cent forthcoming when they were recalled ! The latter will apply to *few* other articles with which the Home Guard has been issued.

Nevertheless, there never was a less expensive National Defence Force.

Courses

In 1942 week-end courses were held at Highworth, the subjects taught being : spigot mortar and Northover, L.M.G., section leading and Sten Gun. The courses were well attended, as were most courses run for Home Guard, especially the week-end courses held at Bulford.

The basis of all the training in the Battalion was to make every man proficient with the weapons he was to use, and in fieldcraft.

Weapon Training

Towards the end of 1942 a small amount of ·300 ammunition was available and most of the rifles were zeroed. There was a lack of foresights, but the lateral error was corrected.

Rifle Meetings

In 1943, the Commanding Officer presented a Challenge Cup for the best shooting company, and it was decided to run a Battalion rifle meeting. Cups were presented by Chiseldon, Wroughton, Blunsdon, Cricklade, Highworth, Wootton Bassett and the Adjutant. The meeting took place on 10th and 17th October, and was a great success. Maj.-Gen. H. O. Curtis, C.B., D.S.O., M.C., was a spectator on the first day, and on the final day Col. Lord Roundway, C.M.G., D.S.O., M.V.O., presented the prizes. The winners of the Commanding Officer's Cup were Chiseldon, who had fired consistently well all through. They also won cups for Match I (Application 200 yards), Match III (Application 300 yards) and Match IV (Inter-Section Match). Wroughton were runners-up ; they won Match VI (Sten Gun). Purton were third, and L/Corp. Woodward, of that Company, won the Individual Championship. Wanborough were fourth, and won Match II (snapshooting). Highworth won the Non-Championship Match (spigot mortar).

The rifle meeting for 1944 took place on 8th and 15th October, and again proved an outstanding success.

·22 Shooting

The Battalion became members of the Society of Miniature Range Clubs in August 1942, but were unable to compete in national competitions due to the wide dispersal of the Battalion and transport difficulties.

A cup was put up for competition during " Wings for Victory " Week in 1943. Five officers and other ranks tied, all gaining the highest possible score of 100. At the shoot-off, Corp. Bampton, of " L " Company, won the Cup.

An Inter-Company League was run during the winter of 1943-44. Teams were of ten, and two fresh members had to be included each week. Companies fired on their own range. Wroughton won the League, and retained an unbeaten record.

Camps

During 1942 many men had been disappointed by the news that the Salisbury Plain District Camp was cancelled, but with the help of the 1st M.T. Battalion, K.R.R.C., a Battalion camp was held at Hannington Bridge from 13th-20th September. Maj. J. M. Farrant was Camp Commandant, and over 100 spent a very beneficial week, both from the health and training point of view.

In 1943 the camp at Hannington Bridge was pitched early in June, and was available every week-end. The week's camp was held from July 31st to 7th August, and a very enjoyable time was spent. Maj. Farrant again was Camp Commandant, and " H " Travelling Wing assisted in the instruction. Four hundred and ten officers and other ranks spent either a week-end or a week in camp.

The camp in 1944 was again held at Hannington Bridge, and was pitched in May, commencing with a week-end camp at Whitsuntide.

It was not surprising that attendances were not very large, as all the preliminary arrangements for " D " Day caused all ranks to put in extra time on guards and pickets. Many had to work longer hours, but about 300 spent a week-end or longer under canvas. The week's camp was held from August 5th to 12th. About 40 attended, and the numbers were raised by members of the R.A.F. from a maintenance unit joining. " H " Travelling Wing provided the instruction, and a thoroughly enjoyable time was spent. Whilst in camp, one company had the good fortune to enjoy a first-rate lecture on airborne troops, and also a trip in a glider.

Exercises

These were many and varied, and included some with the 1st M.T. Battalion, K.R.R.C., and later the U.S.A. troops.

Exercises " Hawk ", " Runner " and " White Horse " were perhaps the three most valuable and interesting.

Exercise " Hawk " was a series of " surprise " exercises carried out in platoon or company areas during some of their parade periods in February 1943.

The main object was to " test the speed of reaction to news of the landing of paratroops, and the passing of information to headquarters and units concerned."

" Incidents " were arranged by Battalion Headquarters to take place in areas where it was known platoons and companies were parading. As a rule, information of the " incident " was taken by officers and/or N.C.O.s of a neighbouring company, and given to the Police or other local person, with a request to pass it on to Home Guards. The officers or N.C.O.s then acted as umpires or enemy, as the occasion required.

In addition, the Battalion Commander and/or his Adjutant were also on the scene to observe reaction and action taken.

The exercise was realistic, instructive, entertaining and commendably executed.

Exercise " Runner " was to test out the organisation of the communication within the Battalion, in the event of telephone and main road communications being disrupted, with special attention to message writing, verbal messages, passing of important information quickly, and organisation of Battalion and Company Headquarters signals.

"White Horse " was of a more comprehensive nature, although it involved only four companies of this Battalion—" H ", " I ", "D ", and " G ". The exercise was to try out U.S.A. troops in the rôle of an airborne division in an attack on Swindon, and to test the Home Guard in their various rôles.

CEREMONIAL PARADES
Home Guard Anniversary Parades

As companies were so dispersed, Battalion parades were few and far between. In fact, the only occasions were the birthday parades held in Swindon, in conjunction with the 5th, 11th and 13th Battalions, and Battalion rifle meetings.

The first of the former was held on 16th May 1943, when the parade state showed 30 officers and 496 other ranks on parade. This did not include representatives from the Ashton Keynes (" A " Company), Cricklade (" B " Company), Highworth (" D " Company) or Wootton Bassett (" H " Company), as birthday parades were being held in these areas, nor from " J ", " K ", " L " and " M " Companies.

Companies formed up in battle platoons at various points in Old Swindon, and fell in the rear of the procession as it passed, with sub-artillery, signals and first aid units in rear of companies.

The salute was taken by Maj.-Gen. H. O. Curtis, C.B., D.S.O., M.C., in Regent Circus.

The route of march was some three miles long, and the parade was completed without a single hitch or casualty, which reflected great credit on all concerned.

The Commanding Officer's Special Order of the Day follows :

HOME GUARD ANNIVERSARY PARADE
SWINDON, 16TH MAY 1943
SPECIAL ORDER OF THE DAY BY THE
COMMANDING OFFICER

To ALL COMPANIES :

Yesterday we had 30 officers and 496 other ranks on parade. It was a first class show and the District Commander told me personally how very pleased he was with the splendid appearance of the Battalion. I want to thank EVERYONE, especially my company commanders, on the good result achieved, as I am fully aware and greatly appreciate that an immense amount of trouble had been taken to reach such a high standard.

That our standard of efficiency is equally high if and when we are called on to fight in the field I am pretty confident.

But let no one think we have reached the peak of perfection. I know there is much hard work to be done in your civil employment, but I do however appeal to EVERYONE to do their utmost to see that the standard now reached does not decline. From now on the duties of the Home Guard increase in importance and the safety of ENGLAND is largely in our hands. Let us *all* do our best until the final whistle blows.

I know you are all proud of yourselves.

I am proud to be your Commanding Officer.

(Signed) A. W. PARSONS,
Lt.-Col.,

Highworth, 17 *May* 1943.　　Commanding 9th Wiltshire Battalion Home Guard.

A similar parade with similar results was held on 14th May 1944, when the salute was taken by Lt.-Gen. Sir R. D. Stephens, K.C.B., C.M.G., D.L.

The parade state on this occasion showed that 26 officers and 334 other ranks paraded, and again did not include representatives from " A ", " B ", " H ", " L " and" M " Companies.

The Commanding Officer's Order of the Day follows :

HOME GUARD ANNIVERSARY PARADE

SWINDON, 14TH MAY 1944

SPECIAL ORDER OF THE DAY BY THE
COMMANDING OFFICER

TO ALL COMPANIES :

To mark the fourth anniversary of the formation of the Home Guard we had 26 officers and 334 other ranks on parade in the march through Swindon yesterday. As last year, the general bearing of the Battalion was a fine sight. It fully maintained and possibly improved upon last year's magnificent effort.

I send my congratulations and grateful thanks to EVERYONE, and especially to my company commanders, for having kept up such a high standard. The King in his message to us says : " To the tasks which lie ahead the Home Guard will be enabled to make a full contribution," and further : " To all of you I would like to express my appreciation of your past service and my confidence that you will continue to carry on in the same high spirit of patriotism that you have always shown, until the day of victory."

I am absolutely confident that every member of the 9th Battalion, which I have the honour to command, will do his best to overcome any difficulties which may confront him, and so help to maintain to the utmost that confidence which His Majesty places in the Home Guard. This can only be achieved by the whole-hearted co-operation of each one of us, whatever rank is held in the Battalion in which we are all proud to serve.

(Signed) A. W. PARSONS,
Lt.-Col.,
Commanding 9th Wiltshire Battalion Home Guard.

Highworth, 15 May, 1944.

" Salute the Soldier "

On Saturday 1st July 1944, 101 officers and other ranks represented the Battalion on a march past in connection with " Salute the Soldier " Campaign.

Stand down Parade in London

A ceremonial parade took place in London on 3rd December. Corp. W. Bull, of Highworth, Pte. A. S. Curtis, of Cricklade, and Pte. S. A. Saunders, of Wanborough Company, attended the parade, and represented the 9th Battalion.

Battalion Stand down

Due to the scattered area of the Battalion, which covers more than 150 square miles, a central stand down parade was impossible. As it was considered rather an ambitious programme to visit all the thirteen companies in one day, five of them had their final parades on Sunday, 26th November ; four more were addressed during the week prior to Sunday, 3rd December, and the last four on the appointed day. As well as being more convenient, it was also more appropriate, as the companies had been more or less independent units from the beginning.

500 Joined Up

The companies were drawn up in villages and areas for which they had been responsible, and many who might have had cause to be thankful for the existence of the Home Guard, came to add their sincere, if unspoken, tribute to that expressed by the Commanding Officer, Lt.-Col. A. W. Parsons, C.M.G., D.S.O., who was accompanied by Battalion Second in Command, Maj. N. L. Whatley, and the Adjutant, Capt. E. J. Hawxwell.

Among the spectators were several ex-Home Guardsmen, including servicemen on leave. In this connection it is interesting to note that within the last two years over 500 of the 9th Battalion have joined the Forces. Out of a total strength of 2,120 officers and other ranks over 50 per cent were on parade. Pride of place must be given to the Wanborough Company, who mustered 90 per cent, followed closely by the Clyffe Pypard Company (89 per cent).

After reading a Special Order of the Day for the Home Guard by Gen. Sir H. E. Franklin, Com.-in-Chf. of the Home Forces, the Commanding Officer added his thanks for the fine spirit of co-operation, thanking especially company commanders and the commanders of the outlying platoons, whose task had been no easy one.

He said how proud they had all been to belong to the 9th Battalion, and to have had the privilege of wearing the badge of the county regiment—a regiment with such glorious traditions—and he was aware of how much the regiment appreciated the high standard reached by the Home Guard, and the way in which the Home Guard upheld the honour of that badge.

The Battalion had a great reputation for efficiency, and he hoped that they would uphold this by handing in all kit promptly.

He wished all ranks the very best of luck and hoped that the grand spirit of Home Guard comradeship would be maintained in their future life. He ended by saying how proud he was to have been their Commanding Officer.

10TH BATTALION WILTSHIRE HOME GUARD

The Genesis of the Local Defence Volunteers

By 14th May 1940 the many ex-officers who had been " sitting on the steps of the War Office " and whose offers of service had been somewhat tersely turned down, had realised that this was to be a " Young Men's War ", that Dunkirk might have occurred even if they had still been serving and had resigned themselves to the inevitable.

To them, Mr. Eden's broadcast with the 9 o'clock news came like the sound of a trumpet to the old war-horse and it was not surprising that there was a race before breakfast next morning to the Pewsey Police Station, which was won by Col. Bell by a short head, Lt.-Col. Keith and Maj. Coles tying for second place.

For a few days nothing happened, but on 22nd May Col. Bell informed me that it had been decided to form a Local Defence Volunteer Battalion in the district, of which half was to be at Pewsey, whilst I was to raise a company from the villages of Oare, Wootton Rivers, Wilcot and Alton Barnes.

Then it was a case of Col. Bell and myself (no transport being available) going over each day to the ordnance depot at Ludgershall to draw such rifles, clothing and equipment as we could get hold of. We soon learnt that almost each item was in a separate building and that we must get through before 12 noon, when everything stopped for tea or its equivalent and we thought that we had done rather well, but we could not get any pull-through weights for love or money.

The evenings were spent holding recruiting meetings with very good results as almost everyone wanted to do what he could. In one instance the command of the local platoon was taken over by the vicar of the parish, but with the coming of Sunday parades and being somewhat elderly, the Rev. Jenkins had regretfully to hand over his platoon to a younger man.

22 May 1940

Early Days

It is generally thought that this Battalion was from its inauguration part of the Marlborough Battalion, but it would appear from S.P.A. Local Defence Volunteers General Instructions No. 1, issued 22nd May 1940, that this is not quite correct, and apparently the formation of a battalion at Marlborough was not even considered at the outset.

The following are brief extracts :

1. *Area.* The S.P.A. for the Local Defence Volunteers comprises the whole of Wiltshire. The Salisbury-Pewsey Zone coincides with the Police divisions of Everleigh, Pewsey and Salisbury, and Amesbury, and these two divisions will be commanded by sub-area commanders.

| Pewsey Sub-area | Lt.-Col. W. C. Heward Bell |
| Salisbury Sub-area | Maj.-Gen. W. P. H. Hill |

2. *Organisation.* Sub-area will be sub-divided into company, platoon and section districts with company and platoon commanders and section leaders. A section will consist of 7-10 men. There will be no officers or N.C.O.s and no pay or other emoluments.

3. *Recruiting and Enrolments.* Immediate steps will be taken to enrol volunteers through the Police. This must be treated as very urgent. Only thoroughly reliable men to be enrolled. There will be no punishment except dismissal. No allowances can be given for clerical or other assistance.

4. *Establishment.* The establishment for the zone for the present is 800. Pewsey Sub-area is allotted 300 and Salisbury Sub-area 500 men.

5. *Equipment and Uniform.* The following uniform and equipment will be issued :

	Salisbury Sub-area	*Pewsey Sub-area*
Denim Overalls	375	225
Caps, F.S.	500	300
Rifles	250	150
Ammunition	2,500 rounds	1,500 rounds

Rifles to be kept under lock and key by section commanders or other permanent guard. All ranks to wear Local Defence Volunteer brassards on right arm above elbow. (The remaining instructions deal with the duties to be done by the Local Defence Volunteers.)

(Signed) R. F. A. HOBBS, Brig.-Gen.
Zone Organiser,
Salisbury-Pewsey Zone.

General Instructions No. 2, mainly dealing with the rôle of the Local Defence Volunteers were similarly issued on 29th May.

The foregoing gives some idea of how small the Local Defence Volunteers were to have been.

The Salisbury-Pewsey Zone only lasted for about ten days, as Brig.-Gen. Hobbs was moved to another command, and when Gen. Sir Francis Gathorne Hardy, G.C.B., G.C.V.O., took over Zone Organiser for Wiltshire, his first step was to form a Local Defence Volunteer unit at Marlborough and it was thus that the Marlborough Half-Battalion and Pewsey Half-Battalion came into being.

31 *May* 1940

Col. Bell telephoned 15.00 hours : " Road-blocks to be put on to-night, roads to be blocked with carts and any motor failing to halt, to be fired on with shotguns."

At 21.00 hours this was altered to " All cars and pedestrians to be stopped. Identity cards to be examined and if cars fail to stop, firing to be directed at the wheels."

Of course this entailed a fresh lot of orders to the different guards. Having made up the detail of duties for the next ten days'

2 *June* 1940

we got " All road-blocks cancelled till further orders," but next day,

3 *June* 1940

" All road-blocks to be re-instituted."

Perhaps what was worse than these changes of orders was the shortage of red lamps and shotguns, as different platoons were on duty and the road-blocks in different places each night, entailing lamps being moved where required each day and guns being borrowed as and when necessary.

By 3rd June a fifth platoon had come into being at Clench, where the employees of Capt. Laye's racing stables had expressed a desire to join No. 3 Company in preference to becoming an outlying detachment of the Marlborough Company. The majority lived within the Marlborough area, but as Clench included the somewhat isolated landing ground at Overton Heath, the alteration of boundary was readily concurred in.

8 *June* 1940

Drew 10 dummies, 5 petrol coupons and 80 suits of denim canvas. The last mostly the size of a London policeman. Some of the trousers were over 4 feet long in the leg and we actually got one man inside one leg.

11 *June* 1940

Two unshaven strangers speaking broken English, studying a map, in possession of a large sum of money but boots worn out, were reported at closing time at the White Hart, Oare. Information received too late to apprehend them, so telephoned particulars to Marlborough.

12 *June* 1940

Marlborough reported that suspects had been duly apprehended and handed over to Intelligence.

15 *August* 1940

We Become Home Guards

Under A.C.1. 924 of to-day's date, we cease to be Local Defence Volunteers and are now called Home Guards, or more correctly the Home Guard. As such, we form part of the Regular Army and have the same powers of arrest, etc.

Personnel have to be reasonably physically fit, between 17 and 65 years of age, sign the dotted line on Army Form W 3,066 and will still be called volunteers.

In addition to the present issues, we are to get service respirators (as one cannot handle arms or shoot in a civilian gas mask), eyeshields, anti-gas outfit, field dressings, steel helmets, greatcoats, boots, gaiters, belts, haversacks and two brassards marked " Home Guard ".

Blankets will be issued, 1 for every 2 men and ground sheets, 1 for every 4 men.

Sections are to be made up of 25 men and the badges of rank will be

    Battalion Commander 3 dark blue stripes on the shoulder straps

    Company Commander 2 ,, ,, ,, ,, ,, ,, ,,

    Platoon Commander 1 ,, ,, ,, ,, ,, . ,, ,,

Section commanders will wear sergeants' chevrons and squad commanders corporal's chevrons.

The pay conditions remain the same and the mileage rate for cars over 10 h.p. is still 3d. per mile.

Paragraph 24 (e) of this A.C.1. reads : " It has been represented that the owners of vans, etc., may be willing to place their vehicles at the disposal of the Home Guard to convey men and stores. Advantage should be taken of these offers and the mileage rates laid down above (3d. per mile) may be drawn."
18 *August* 1940

The Battle of Marlborough

With a view to testing the defence of Marlborough, it was arranged that the Oare and District Company Home Guard and some Canadian Bren Gun Carriers (representing tanks) together with the Lockeridge Company Home Guard would attack that town to-day.

The first thing to be done from the attackers point of view, was to ascertain how Granham Hill (which is the key to the situation) was being held, so motor-cycle scouts were immediately pushed out for this purpose.

To our great surprise, they sent back word that this steep ridge which over-looks the south side of the town, was *not* being held. The tanks were immediately pushed forward to this point, whence there is a sunken road that should take them down to within a few yards of the road-block at Cow Bridge, practically unobserved.

At the same time, the Oare, Alton, Wilcot and Stanton Platoons were sent forward to work along the ridge and take up positions, whilst the attack from the west by the Lockeridge Company developed.

Meanwhile, the Wootton Rivers Platoon was to work along the edge of Saver-nake Forest, driving in any outposts, if necessary.

On reaching the waterworks at 11.15 hours they found them unguarded, so put up a red flag and poster

" WATERWORKS DESTROYED "

They then went on to the pumping station and finding this unguarded, up went another red flag and poster

" PUMPING STATION DESTROYED 11.40 hours "

Whilst this was going on, the Clench Platoon had got forward unobserved into the outskirts of the town by swimming the river but penetrating further, they found a strong party of the enemy in front of them. They retraced their steps, found some boats and floated down stream a certain distance, then landed again and moved forward unobserved into the yard of the Ailesbury Arms Hotel, opposite the Town Hall.

At 11.55 hours the commander of this platoon having collected his men to-gether, dashed across the road to the Town Hall and up went another poster,

" WE HAVE CAPTURED YOUR WATERWORKS
WE HAVE DESTROYED THE PUMPING STATION
and we have now
BURNT DOWN YOUR TOWN HALL "

Fortunately the cease fire was due at 12 noon, but from thence onwards Granham Hill has formed part of the town's defences and an alternative water supply has been laid on.

6 Sept. 1940

At 23.15 hours the code word was received directing " Strictest vigilence to be observed and Home Guards to be in readiness to turn out at 15 minutes notice. Only essential services such as milking to go on." . This was passed on to platoons. Col. Humfrey, commanding Wilcot Platoon turned all his men out and made them sleep in the village hall, much to the annoyance of the A.R.P. warden, who complained to the Police and in turn the Police sergeant rang me up threatening to prosecute the Home Guard. On receipt of a letter that was signed by all the leading inhabitants of the village, the appointment of the warden as a special constable was cancelled and the Police sergeant was shortly afterwards moved to another station.

8 Sept. 1940

Situation modified, but guards to remain on duty till 08.00 hours. Had to arrange that chauffeurs, gardeners, carters, etc., did the last relief, so that the milkers could get away.

29 Nov. 1940

Numbered Battalions

The Home Guard battalions in Wiltshire have now been numbered and we have now become the 10th Home Guard Battalion, Wiltshire Regiment.

25 Dec. 1940

Christmas Day

The night guards were performed by the officers and farmers so that their employees should enjoy Christmas.

20 Jan. 1941

Battle Dress and Steel Helmets

Received 107 suits of battle dress to-day, just as well as it has been snowing a lot and greatcoats are coming through very slowly. Steel Helmets are also starting to arrive but without chin straps.

25 March 1941

Recognition Identities

A hundred and seventy-seven of these very secret emblems, that have to be kept sealed and under lock and key, were issued to-day to platoon commanders. Then came an order that they must be kept at Company Headquarters, as they were so hush-hush. The joke is that the Regulars are wearing them on manoeuvres.

22 April 1941

Our first conference at Bulford.

Northern Sub-area

The Battalion has now come under the command of Officer Commanding Northern Sub-area, Col. J. M. Hamilton, D.S.O. (He was a subaltern with me at Lucknow.)

18 *May* 1941
Extract from Southern Command Orders
The following appointments have been approved by the G.O.C.-in-C. Southern Command and will take effect from 1 Feb. 1941.

Douglas Coles, T.D., Maj. (retired)	To be Maj.
Cyril Henry Hunt	,, ,, Capt.
William Sidney John Goodman	,, ,, Lt.
Ronald George Cooke	,, ,, Lt.
John Vivian Strong	,, ,, Lt.
Warwick Neville Whittle	,, ,, Lt.
William Godfrey Newton, M.C., Lt.-Col. (retired)	,, ,, Maj.
James Drogo Montagu, C.B.E.	,, ,, Capt.
Harold Victor Robbins	,, ,, Lt.
Oscar Madley Peall	,, ,, Lt.
George Theodore Elphinstone Keith, D.S.O., O.B.E., Lt.-Col. (retired)	,, ,, Maj.
Lord Edward Hambly Humfrey, Lt.-Col. (retired)	,, ,, Capt.
Leslie Allan Wroth	,, ,, Maj.
Charles Bryan Draper, Capt. (retired)	,, ,, Capt.
Wilfrid Edward Cave	,, ,, Lt.
James Arthur Ernest Ryding	,, ,, Lt.
Charles Ernest Scott	,, ,, Lt.
Donald McLeod	,, ,, Lt.
Harry Sykes	,, ,, Lt.
Albert Victor Moore	,, ,, 2/Lt.

7 *July* 1941
·300 Rifles
What with Lewis Guns, Browning Automatics, Tommy Guns, rifles and revolvers, we have now quite a variety of arms but to-day we have had to hand in the balance of our ·303s, receiving ·300s in exchange, plus two ·303s for practice purposes.

To distinguish the ·300s they have all to be painted with a red band.

1 *August* 1941
The Harvest
Command of an agricultural unit during harvest time requires a lot of tact, but the encouragement of the idea that a day off occasionally means a weeks better work, has good results and the weekly tactical exercise on Sundays, especially if we can raise some blank, is usually well attended.

19 *August* 1941
Emergency Rations (See also 30 May 1943)
Went down to Col. Bell's to-day with the large trailer to draw No. 3 Company's rations. Two hundred and eight tins of meat, 432 packets of biscuits, 8 1/6 pounds of chocolate, 154 tins of meat, 25 packets of tea, 19 pounds of sugar, and 25 tins of jam.

According to the A.C.1. they should have been held at the police station, but having no room, Company commanders have to accommodate. Perhaps the issue may have been a wise precaution in the towns, but as each village has a reserve of 14 days flour, groceries, etc., and can obtain plenty of meat and vegetables locally in an emergency, we do not really need them. They will want turning over and unless kept under lock and key will vanish.

21 *August* 1941

Northover Projectors

We received the first of these much maligned drainpipes to-day, but we think they are quite useful weapons. They were issued originally for throwing S.I.P. grenades. Sometimes they did, sometimes they did not and not infrequently the bottle of phosphorus burst in the barrel with a flamenwerfer effect, but seldom would they burst on impact as the ground was too soft. Also they often misfired, but this was mainly a question of keeping a wire in the nipple and the caps and charges dry.

7 *Sept.* 1941

Capt. W. G. Bowditch, M.C., D.C.M., Wiltshire Regiment, appointed Adjutant and Quartermaster.

Nov. 1941

Lettering of Companies

During November all companies were lettered " A ", " B ", " C ", " D " instead of being Nos. 1, 2, 3, 4, Companies.

At the end of November Salisbury Plain Area (S.P.A.) changed its title to Salisbury Plain District (S.P.D.).

19 *Jan.* 1942

The Spigot Mortar

To-day saw the issue of our first spigot mortar.

Whether it was the fact that two Home Guard units had fired what they thought was a dummy bomb, weighing 28 pounds through the roof of their drill hall, whether it was the stories that the live bomb had a danger zone of 1,000x and the best range to fire the mortar was 75x, or whether it was the heavy weight of the mortar and its kick of 18 tons, that frightened everyone beforehand, I do not know, but at the beginning it was an unpopular weapon and teams soon got tired of firing dummies and of digging them out. When live ammunition arrived however, it rapidly became popular and it was found to be a very accurate weapon that could be relied on. It was not long before we had fixed up concrete mountings where necessary and (with R.A.F. permission) we got in a lot of good practices on landing grounds in the area. Usually the target was only an empty petrol tin at 500x, but every shot was within 10 yards and direct hits were frequent. The difficulty of finding the range was overcome by means of a fixed base and pointer tables.

Later we did a good deal of indirect firing with very accurate results and platoons got so fond of the weapon that they mounted them on trailers whenever possible, carrying the mortar with the legs fixed in, so that it could be lifted off and brought into action quickly. In all we had 38 spigot mortars, mostly mobile before Stand Down took place.

22 *Jan.* 1942

A.C.I. 151/1942 issued to-day, cancels the possibility of retiring from the Home Guard by 14 days notice, as from 16th February next, but members will still be able to apply for discharge owing to sickness, change of conditions or hardship.

Also, it legislates that if called out to resist actual or apprehended invasion, men may have to live away from their homes during the danger period.

That members may be called on to do 48 hours per 4 weeks and in default be liable on summary conviction to be imprisoned or fined up to £10 or both, but it is left to the discretion of company commanders to decide how many hours an individual can reasonably do and submit that 24 hours per 4 weeks should be aimed at.

Furthermore, that no prosecutions will be undertaken without the consent of the G.O.C.-in-C., and if any Home Guard fails to deliver up any equipment, etc., issued to him, he will be guilty of an offence.

Should compulsory enrolment be ordered in the district, the Ministry of Labour can order any man between the ages of 18 and 51 to join the Home Guard.

Only about 1 per cent elected to retire gracefully from this Battalion, and those who did go, were those whom we did not want.

Billeting

Although farms that are Home Guard headquarters, are normally exempt from being commandeered as billets, one does not like to refuse and yesterday when approached by an A.P.M. of a division doing manoeuvres, to use my granary for a divisional prisoner of war cage and the chicken-rearing house for interrogating prisoners, I rapidly assented.

During the night no less than 74 prisoners were brought in, accompanied by the usual requests for hot water, loaning blankets, etc., so when this morning our guests departed and stated that " the corps prisoner of war cage would be coming in to-day," something had to be done about it, with the result that one of the yellow triangles bearing the word " Gas ", was duly hung on the stable door.

Later the corps cage party arrived and the following conversation was heard : " Ere Bill, we can't stop here, we shall have to wear respirators the whole time," and shortly afterwards they moved on to another farm.

It was not till afterwards that I realised that they might have sent for a decontamination squad, squirted carbolic over my roses and even have insisted on me being sprayed.

1 *Feb.* 1942

Anno Domini

Alas the order for the discharge of all who are over 65 has arrived and I shall be losing Lt.-Col. Humfrey, M.C., Commanding Wilcot Platoon who has helped me very considerably and acted as Second in Command.

Also Commander Baker, R.N., Commanding Wootton Rivers Platoon. He always refers to " watch keeping ", port and starboard, etc., but he is very keen and hardworking.

121

Likewise old Gordon, an ex-jockey of bygone days, who knows every gate in the county and has done valuable work, hacking over the downs every day and reporting unusual circumstances.

Fortunately I have been able to obtain the services of Capt. Hay-Will, M.C. who has come to live at Wootton Rivers and Capt. Hon. R. C. Boyle, M.C., who has been doing air warden during the week in London and helping the Wilcot Platoon at week-ends and who will now be able to give his full time to Wilcot.

6 *Feb.* 1942

Pikes

With a view to frightening Hitler, Lord Croft has gone and issued pikes to the Home Guard, consisting of an antiquated bayonet, stuck into a piece of 1½ inch iron piping. Bayonet 17 inches and pipe 3 feet 9 inches, also some bludgeons. (I have refused to accept them, as if needs be, the men would do far better work with a hay prong.)

9 *March* 1942

Col. Bell and I attended Gen. Gathorne Hardy's last conference at Marlborough at which he announced that he was ceasing to be in charge of the Wiltshire Home Guard Zone as from 1st April 1942.

26 *March* 1942

Col. Bell broke it to me gently that under the age clause he had got to retire and I had to take over command of the Battalion as from the same date.

1 *April* 1942

The Other Companies

To bring in any events that affected the other companies, or Battalion Head-quarters prior to my taking over from Col. Bell they are inserted here.

No. 1 Pewsey Company was commanded by Maj. D. Coles, T.D. from its formation, till like Col. Bell, Col. Humfrey and Commander Baker he had to retire for age, but both he and Col. Bell wishing to do what they could, accepted appointments as ammunition officers with the rank of lieutenant. (Col. Bell in this Battalion, and Maj. Coles with the Marlborough Battalion.) Thus on my taking over, the list of company and platoon Commanders was as follows :

" A " Company

Company Commander :
    Maj. C. A. K. Ludbrook
Platoon Commanders : Lt. R. G. Cooke, Lt. J. V. Strong, Lt. W. N. Whittle, Lt. W. S. J. Goodman, Sgt. J. S. Haines.

" B " Company

Company Commander :
    Maj. W. G. Newton, M.C.
Second in Command :
    Capt. J. D. Montagu, C.B.E.
Platoon Commanders : Sgt. G. Gray,

Sgt. J. F. C. Tasker, Sgt. F. H. Rutter, Lt. A. N. Clarke, Lt. W. A. Horsell, Lt. H. V. Robbins, Sgt. A. L. Mousley.

" C " Company

Company Commander :
    The Hon. R. C. Boyle, M.C.
Second in Command :
    Capt. N. G. Hay-Will, M.C.
Platoon Commanders : Sgt. R. Habgood, Lt. O. M. Peall, Lt. S. C. Pope, Sgt. H. G. Smith, 2/Lt. W. H. Maidment, Sgt. W. Ralph.

122

"D" Company

Company Commander :
Maj. L. A. Wroth

Second in Command :
Capt. C. B. Draper

Platoon Commanders : Lt. A. V. Moore, C.S.M. A. H. Wheeler, Lt. D. McLeod, Lt. W. E. Cave, Lt. J. A. E. Ryding, Lt. H. Sykes, Lt. A. Y. Semple

In addition to the above, there were certain detachments at Netheravon Aerodrome, Tidworth Ordnance and a party on special duties at Shipton Bellinger, which entailed this village (which is actually in Hampshire) being incorporated in the Battalion area. To all intents and purposes, the Battalion area coincided with the Pewsey Rural District, excluding the parish of Burbage (which was allotted to Marlborough defences) but including Stanton St. Bernard (in the Devizes area) as it was not desirable to have two different battalions responsible for the defence of the Alton Landing Ground.

Likewise the Overton Heath Landing Ground was ceded from Marlborough to this Battalion.

Thus the Battalion, extended from Clench in the north to Figheldean in the south, as the crow flies, 11 miles, but by road 16 miles, and from Stanton in the west to Chute in the east, 15 miles direct and 21 miles by road, in all the area being over 170 square miles.

1 April 1942

O.P.s have now to be manned 19.00 hours till 1 hour after blackout and 2 hours before sunrise till ½ hour after sunrise. During strong moons, 03.30 hours till ½ hour after sunrise.

Owing to the shortage of watches and alarm clocks most O.P.s are going to do the usual 2 hours on and 4 hours off.

2 April 1942

Expected Invasion

21.25 hours. Col. Ashburner (O.C. Searchlight) asked me to come up urgently to Oare House, and showed me a message stating that a raid on Southern England was likely to-night, that all his men were standing to and priming grenades.

Placed company and platoon headquarters on alert but did not issue grenades.

Presumably the 400 troop-carrying planes that are stated to be in Normandy are tuning up, but Sector knew nothing about it, so leaving G. M. Young on the telephone and trusting that it would not filter through the " usual channels " before dawn, we had a peaceful night.

22 April 1942

Conscription

With the arrival of compulsory service in the Home Guard, A.C.1. 924/40 (irreverantly known as the Home Guard Bible) has had to be revised and to-day A.C.1. 872/42 has made its appearance.

Under the National Service (Armed Forces) Act, men between the ages of 17 and 51 can be directed into the Home Guard to fill any vacancies in the establish-ment of unit.

Men who are over 51 may still enlist voluntarily for the duration of the emergency or until the age of 65 years. Up to 51, they are to be recorded as enlisted " until called up for service ".

The equipment has been increased by 4 more anti-gas eyeshields, 1 pair anklets, 1 set web braces and pouches and 1 suit of battle dress (with badges of rank, titles, etc.).

27 *April* 1942

Devizes Conference

This month's zone conference of battalion commanders, was held at Devizes Town Hall, Lord Roundway having succeeded Gen. Sir F. Gathorne Hardy as Zone Commander.

28 *April* 1942

Move to Pewsey Wharf

Heretofore Battalion headquarters has been Col. Bell's house in Pewsey, but the increase of staff, bringing in its train the inevitable increase of correspondence, has entailed our moving into more spacious quarters, and to-day we have migrated to The Bungalow at The Wharf, Pewsey despite the protestations of the Billeting Officer who wanted the bungalow himself.

10 *May* 1942

Bogus Fifth Columnists

On a tactical exercise to-day, the officer in command Headquarters guard reported that they had a D.R. in the guard-room as his papers were not in order, would I see him as the Adjutant and Intelligence Officer were engaged, so I had him marched in. On being asked where he had come from, he replied " Heil Hitler," so he was immediately marched out. Five minutes later the Police arrived and took delivery. It was the Sector Intelligence Officer dressed up, and he spent the rest of the day in a Police cell, all proof that he was the Intelligence Officer having been carefully removed.

18 *May* 1942

South Wiltshire Sub-area

North Wiltshire Sub-area having been done away with, we were to-day transferred to the administration of South Wiltshire Sub-area (Col. Flemming).

11 *July* 1942

Sten Carbines

To-day we have received 37 Sten Carbines, or Guns as they are usually called.

A wonderful little 9 m.m. weapon, that costs very little and is being turned out by mass production, in place of the Tommy-guns that we had to hand in last April. It has, I understand been christened " The Woolworth ".

(In all we received 255 Stens before Stand Down, despite numerous pleas that as they were only a short range weapon, they were more suitable for street fighting than for use in the country.)

13 *Oct.* 1942
The Smith Gun
Perhaps the best way of describing this gun, is to call it a cross between a gun and an umbrella, as it consists of a gun and limber with disc wheels and for firing, the gun is turned over on its side.

In this position, the gun has an all round traverse on the axle, whilst the off side umbrella like wheel affords overhead protection to the firer.

We received an issue of 5 guns on 13th Sept. and wishing to learn how to use the gun, a number of officers attended a demonstration at Larkhill on 19th Sept. 1942, where Home Guards had gathered from far and wide to see it fired, but alas there was only one gun on view and its striker refused to function, however we all trooped back to-day and saw several guns in action.

It has been my invariable custom at all lectures, to make those who were present produce their field-dressings, but on this occasion I was caught myself. I had made room for a spectator who was behind me, so that he could see the firing, when suddenly we heard the unwelcome noise of something coming in our direction. Almost simultaneously he gave a shout of pain and he was bleeding badly from the temple, having been hit by a stone or a splinter.

I felt for my field-dressing, but I had got the wrong suit on.

25 *Nov.* 1942
An Adjutant at Last
The increasing amount of clerical work has resulted in Bowditch having to devote almost all his time to " Q " resulting in my having to take the N.C.O.s cadre class and do mostly Adjutant's work for several months, so we were very delighted to see the arrival of Capt. H. Piper this morning.

He is an ex-Hythe instructor and should be very useful.

23 *Feb.* 1943
Command
Maj.-Gen. R. P. Pakenham Walsh, C.B., M.C. has been replaced at S.P.D. by Maj.-Gen. H. O. Curtis, C.B., D.S.O., M.C. to-day.

Feb. 1943
Hawk Exercises
Most of this month has been taken up " Hawking " or going round detachments, in other words handing the first Home Guard that one met in a village " Hawk Exercise ". " A detachment of enemy paratroops has landed at —————. Take action immediately." Of seeing what he did, how long the detachment took to turn out and the action taken.

On the whole, the results were very encouraging and it was perhaps fortunate that two or more incidents did not occur simultaneously as staff officers from S.P.D. and Sub-area Headquarters were also going round painting situations.

1 *March* 1943
Civil Defence Conferences
One of these monthly occurrences took place to-day and on the usual enquiry

as to relation with the Home Guard, we got the usual " Relations with the 10th Battalion could not be better."

Col. Flemming was very insistant that we move our Headquarters into Pewsey, but I managed to stave it off by quoting an order that Home Guard headquarters must be where communications are best.

When there is a show on, one does not want to be bothered with continuous enquiries and disturbances that are adherent to having the Civil Defence and Home Guard headquarters under one roof and we get over this by having an information room, a liaison officer at Civil Defence Headquarters and a private telephone line, whereby the map in Pewsey (which is identical) can be marked up to date.

If I want to see the Chairman of the Civil Defence Committee, it is only two minutes run in a car but we are away from the din of motor-cycles, etc., and if any umpires' cars stop outside The Bungalow, they are very firmly removed by the Corporal of the Guard.

23 *April* 1943

Church Bells

Reminiscent that church bells had been used with effect in the Battle of Lexington, 1775, it was decided that this method of alarm would be used for calling out the Home Guard in the event of invasion.

Of course there were immediate protests from sundry church dignatories, but they were dismissed with the intimation " that there is a war on " and in due course one Home Guard was told off in each village to toll the bell, if ordered to do so by a Police constable, by a Home Guard officer, or if he had personally witnessed a descent of more than 4 enemy parachutists. (It was subsequently discovered that some of our own planes carried more than 4 persons, so the number was increased to 25 parachutists.)

On no account was a bell to be rung because a neighbouring village was tolling its bell, as like the 3-rifle shot alarm signal that travelled down the blockhouses from Mafeking to Capetown in the Boer War, there might be a *feu de joie* of church bells from Lands End to John 'o Groats.

We soon found out that church bells only carried the way the wind was blowing, that the rope was broken or the church door locked, or the man concerned was away at work, so most villages, in addition to their knock-up system, adopted a bugle or car that was driven from one end of the village to the other with the driver's finger on the horn button.

Fortunately it was never necessary to inform the Police that " it had stuck ", though at times they thought that some motorist had had one over the eight.

To-day, it has been announced that whistles, bugles, car horns, thunder flashes and cadets on cycles may be used, but at any rate there must be a house to house knock-up system in each village.

28 *June* 1943

Change of Policy

Whether it was with the arrival of a new G.O.C., Maj.-Gen. H. O. Curtis, C.B., D.S.O., M.C. who took over command of S.P.D. 14th April 1943, or whether it came from still higher authority, we do not know, but at the C.O.s conference to-day, we were greeted with the splendid news that the policy was all changed and in future we were to be·as mobile as possible. Only certain specified towns and tank islands were to be considered as vulnerable points, the 1,000x operational boundary was no more and we were to submit recommendations as to which V.P.s in our area could cease to be considered as such. Could we become mobile ? The answer from the company commanders was " No " because we were already so.

14 *July* 1943

" E " Company

It being the considered opinion of the powers that be, that " D " Company was far too big for one officer to command, the Shipton Bellinger, Tidworth and Ludgershall Platoons, were to-day transferred to a new " E " Company under the command of Maj. J. E. French, M.C.

5 *August* 1943

End of South Wiltshire Sub-area

South Wiltshire Sub-area was abolished on 5th August 1943 and the 10th Battalion then passed under direct administration of Salisbury Plain District.

18 *August* 1943

East Sector

To-day we have been placed under the administration of O.C. Troops Bulford, Col. P. J. N. Ellison, Grenadier Guards, who will be designated O.C. East Sector.

It looks rather like our having to find all the personnel for the Sector Headquarters, being the only unit in the Sector.

22 *Feb.* 1944

Southern Sector

Col. H. St. G. Schomberg, D.S.O., took over Southern Sector, so the Battalion is once more connected up with Salisbury, whence it started.

We were together at the Senior Officers' School.

6 *March* 1944

New G.O.C.

Maj.-Gen. Curtis, has been transferred to Dorset and the command of Salisbury Plain District has been taken over by Maj.-Gen. R. H. Laurie, C.B., C.B.E.

28 *April* 1944

The last of the battalion commanders conferences at Bulford.

These conferences were started by Gen. Gathorne Hardy at Marlborough and when Lord Roundway took over they were continued monthly at Devizes, the Secretary Territorial Association and Home Guard Staff Officer (Col. Drew and later Col. Ellison) being present, but one day the G.I. attended.

Then Sector Commander and the G.O.C. District started to attend and it was not long before the G.O.C. decided that it would be better to meet at S.P.D. Headquarters where representatives of the directorates would be present, so from 27th September 1943 we had to meet at Bulford.

Then it was decided that it was unnecessary for battalion commanders to attend, as the sector commanders were there and so what we called the activities of the C.O.s Union came to an end.

10 *May* 1944
Railway Duties
At last we have something to do that is worth doing, was the general remark when it became known that we were to guard the railway lines.

Railway waiting-rooms were made available at Pewsey, Collingbourne and Ludgershall, whilst the deserted mill at New Mill was made as habitable as circumstances would permit.

We also expected to have a guard at Manningford but that did not materialise. All these guards were connected up by private telephone to Battalion Headquarters over 20 miles of cable being laid for the purpose.

6 *June* 1944
" D " Day
About 22.00 hours to-night we received a cryptic message from the Radio Location Station to the effect that " Parachutists had left, destination unknown, all Home Guards to stand to with arms and ammunition." We went down and saw the Police, who had apparently received the same message through their channels, so passed it on to S.P.D. stating that we had no intention of standing to, till we received orders from them, as if it referred to German paratroops their destination might be anywhere.

It was subsequently ascertained that the information was a garbled account of our paratroops having started for " D " Day.

21 *June* 1944
Orders received to-day for railway guards to be discontinued.

23 *June* 1944
Col. The Duke of Somerset, D.S.O., O.B.E. appointed Wiltshire Home Guard Advisor.

25 *August* 1944
Director General's Conference
Attended a conference at Marlborough to-day to meet Gen. Drew, Director General of the Home Guard, which was mainly on the subject of articles that have been appearing in the more irresponsible newspapers demanding the immediate disbandment of the Home Guard, now that they had nothing to do.

8 *Nov.* 1944
Salisbury Plain District has now changed its name to Salisbury Plain and Dorset District.

26 *Nov.* 1944
The Stand Down Parade

The official date for the Stand Down parades was December 3rd but units could, if they so desired, hold their parades on November 26th, and realising that it would be difficult to obtain a band, that 'busses would be at a premium and inspecting officers would be very scarce on the 3rd, we decided to hold our Battalion parade at 11.30 a.m. on Sunday 26th November, thereby giving companies and platoons the opportunity of holding their own village parades and church services, if they so desired on 3rd December.

We had been lucky in obtaining the services of the Wiltshire Regiment Band, there was to be a march past in Pewsey of all five companies, followed by a talk in the Cinema, photographs, etc.

I had hoped to get Gen. Gathorne Hardy to take the salute at the parade but he had a previous engagement, so I had asked Gen. Laurie instead.

It came somewhat as a shock, when a few days ago, Maj. Boyle came to me saying that he had had a depututation from the Battalion, expressing the wish that I should take its farewell salute instead of any generals. I informed him that I was not prepared to go to the G.O.C. and ask him to stand down, so he went himself and Gen. Laurie kindly assented.

About 650 men marched past and then filed into the Rex Cinema, where everyone had a seat and on the platform were Lt.-Col. Keith, Col. Bell, the ex officers Lt.-Col. Humfrey, Commander Baker, Maj. Coles, Maj. Ludbrook, together with Maj. Boyle and the company commanders.

Maj. Boyle opened up by extolling the virtues of Col. Bell and Col. Keith, finishing up with, " I am indeed sorry for Mrs. Keith whose husband has been out all hours of the day and night for the past four and a half years."

Lt.-Col. Keith began by thanking Maj. Boyle for all that he had said and done, also Gen. Laurie and Col. Schomberg, commanding the Sector, for giving him the privilege of taking the salute (this was cut out by the censors in case it was of use to the enemy) but quoting the Press :

" He began by congratulating the Battalion on the way that it had turned out and marched past, which was a further credit to the very high standard that the Battalion had attained. It had received a Best in Wiltshire Arms Inspection Report, also a similar Transport Condition Report, come out on top in both kinds of spigot mortar firing, beaten all comers at football, had only had one case in the Police Courts, been the most economical battalion in Wiltshire by £200. It was really mobile, having 28 mobile patrols, that could in most cases, fall in in less than 20 minutes and the whole Battalion could be concentrated in an hour. The Battalion had got through its bombing and shooting without a single accident. Its Cadets had surprised everyone. (Here followed an appreciation of what the Cadets had done, finishing with the words :) ' Gentlemen, may I put it to you, that this is mainly due to the good example that you have set the Cadets.' "

How was all this attained ?

" I think the ground was ploughed by L.D.V., the seed was sown by Col. Bell and the original company and platoon commanders, many of whom I am glad to see here to-day. Col. Bell selected good seed, which grew into the Home Guard and as it grew, came Strength, Confidence and Zeal to Improve.

" It was fertilised by Capt. Piper, ridged up by Capt. Wharton, and all the time the two P.S.I.s, Sgt.-Maj. Ward and Sgt.-Maj. Roberts, have been going round day and night with the hoe.

" The result has been a bumper crop, but it is *you* gentlemen, that the crop represents and it has borne fruit, mainly by your patriotism and energy. It is to you that the credit goes and it is only fit, that I should be thanking you, instead of your thanking me.

" Let us congratulate ourselves, that we have done our bit towards the war but remember that even when standing down we can do a bit more. An extra row of potatoes, an extra acre of corn, economy in fuel, salvage, readiness to lend a hand where wanted, letters to relatives in the Forces. They all help and we must go on doing what we can.

" Our thanks are due to many, Mr. Beckett for lending us this cinema so often ; Headquarters S.P.D. and Southern Sector staffs ; the R.A.F. for their wonderful Crash Rescue lectures to every company ; the S.A.S. and the hard worked Territorial Association ; the garrison adjutants at Tidworth and Bulford ; the training officers and the Civil Defence ; the telephone operators whom we have worried day and night ; our friends the Police, who have turned a blind eye so often ; the owners of pigeons ; the farmers, particularly those who have helped with transport and ranges ; the employers of labour who have co-operated, and bringing up the rear of the column, part time Adjutant and full time Quartermaster Capt. Bill Bowditch, who has sweated ink and energy to get us all in the shape of arms, clothing and equipment that we were entitled to, and dare I say it, a bit more.

" I have considered, that all wives, mothers, daughters, sisters, not forgetting those who have typed, telephoned, done first aid and cooked, on our behalf, but also the good ladies who have cleaned our buttons, pressed our trousers and have seen that we got on parade in time, as being a part of the Battalion, that has equally taken its share in the war effort.

" For me, my job is done, but for many of you it is not finished, as I want you to remember not only how your service in the Home Guard has benefitted you personally, but what your service in the Home Guard has meant to the nation, how its formation has allowed our Regular troops to be sent overseas and how it made the Hun change his mind about invasion of this country.

" Above all we must remember—' we were caught unprepared '—' we were caught living in a political atmosphere of self-complacency that there would be no more wars,'—and the League of Nations let us down. Man and boy we have got to bear this in mind. Who knows what the situation will be in twenty years time.

" The Home Guard spirit has got to be kept up, the Home Guard is not abolished—it is in reserve—and in reserve for ever.

" We have got to keep our powder dry, know how to fight and see that our

130

sons know how to fight and despite everything BE READY NEXT TIME. If we are maybe our enemy will again think twice about invading.

"I do ask you, if you have sons or brothers, who are not in the Cadets, to make them join the Cadet movement, as soon as they are old enough.

"Keep them and yourselves, till old age stops you, fighting fit, in mind and in body. Good-bye my comrades and friends, God be with you and the best of luck."

(The King.)

After photographs had been taken, the officers were entertained by Mrs. Keith at the Bouverie Hall, where with a graceful speech, Maj. Boyle handed to Lt.-Col. Bell a silver cup and to Lt.-Col. Keith a silver salver with the signatures of the officers of the Battalion.

List of Officers of the 10th Home Guard Battalion on Standing Down

Battalion Headquarters
Commanding Officer : Lt.-Col. G. T. E. Keith, D.S.O., O.B.E.
Second in Command : Maj. The Hon. R. C. Boyle, M.C., M.B.E.
Adjutant : Capt. B. Wharton
A. & Q. :
Capt. W. G. Bowditch, M.C., D.C.M.
Intelligence Officer : Lt. R. B. Butler
Ammunition Officer :
Lt. W. C. H. Bell, D.S.O.
M.T. Officer : Lt. F. A. Beckett
Signal Officer : 2/Lt. L. B. Cooke

"A" Company
Company Commander : Maj. P. F. Kunkler (vice Maj. C. A. K. Ludbrook)
Second in Command : Capt. R. G. Cooke (O.C. No. 2 Pewsey Platoon)
Company M.O. : Capt. J. C. Byrne
Platoon Commanders: Lt. J. V. Strong, Lt. W. N. Whittle, Lt. G. B. Nicol, Lt. J. S. Haines, Lt. W. S. J. Goodman, 2/Lt. S. G. Glover.

"B" Company
Company Commander : A/Maj. J. D. Montagu, C.B.E. (vice Maj. W. G. Newton, M.C. on leave)

Company M.O. : Capt. L. C. Holland
Platoon Commanders : Lt. G. Gray, Lt. J. F. C. Tasker, 2/Lt. A. G. Dobson, 2/Lt. W. J. Ball, 2/Lt. F. H. Rutter, Lt. A. N. Clarke, 2/Lt. S. G. Waite, 2/Lt. J. C. Pennells, Lt. H. V. Robbins.

"C" Company
Company Commander :
Capt. A. S. Barlow
Second in Command :
Capt. R. Grenfell
Battalion & Company M. O. :
Maj. F. W. Rayment
Platoon Commanders : Lt. R. Habgood, 2/Lt. G. W. P. Cank, Lt. W. H. Maidment, Lt. S. C. Pope.

"D" Company
Company Commander :
Maj. L. A. Wroth, J.P.
Platoon Commanders : Lt. R. F. Bryan, 2/Lt. R. J. Rogers, Lt. A. H. Wheeler, M.M., 2/Lt. M. Barrett, Lt. W. E. Cave, Lt. H. Sykes, 2/Lt. E. F. Harding.

" E " Company

Company Commander :
Maj. J. E. French, M.C.
Second in Command : Capt. A. V. Moore (vice Capt. C. B. Draper)
Company M.O. : Capt. P. D. Abbatt
Platoon Commanders : Lt. E. Foster, 2/Lt. W. G. Kingstone, 2/Lt. G. H. Campion, Lt. F. J. Anquetil, 2/Lt. C. Elgin, Lt. J. Turner, Lt. A. W. Richards, Lt. J. A. E. Ryding, 2/Lt. J. Bull, Lt. A. Y. Semple, 2/Lt. I. E. Davies.

11TH BATTALION WILTSHIRE HOME GUARD

THIS Battalion of the Wiltshire Home Guard came into being in the early days of 1941 when it was considered by the military authorities that each aircraft firm in the Swindon area should become responsible for its own defence. At this time there was one firm organising the production of Stirling Bombers, Messrs. Short Bros. (Rochester & Beford) Ltd., No. 24 Shop, G.W.R., Swindon, and Messrs. Phillips and Powis, Ltd., manufacturing Miles Masters at their aircraft factory at South Marston, the Head Offices of Short Bros. Ltd., being at " The Close ", Stratton St. Margaret. Platoons were formed at G.W.R., South Marston and " The Close ", Stratton St. Margaret and as the staff increased these platoons grew into companies to form " A ", " B " and " C " Companies of the 11th Wiltshire Battalion Home Guard.

Uniforms, arms and equipment were issued by the Wiltshire Territorial Army Association in April 1941 and in May of the same year these three companies were inspected by Gen. Gathorne Hardy.

In June and July 1941 the factories at Sevenhampton, Blunsdon and F.S.2 were completed and commenced production, and " D " Company at Sevenhampton, " E " Company at Blunsdon and " F " Company at F.S.2. were formed.

During this time Messrs. Phillips and Powis Ltd., had raised a Home Guard company from their personnel which formed part of the 9th Wiltshire Battalion Home Guard and Messrs. Plessey Co., had commenced a company at their factory at Kembrey Street, Swindon.

In July 1941 all these factory units were merged into the 11th Wiltshire Battalion Home Guard under the command of Lt.-Col. M. Ormonde Darby, O.B.E., who was then manager at Phillips and Powis Aircraft Factory at South Marston with the Battalion Headquarters at South Marston Factory.

Training was carried out under company arrangements at the various factories after working hours. As the average usual working hours were 10½ hours on day shift and 11 hours on night shift for 7 days a week with one Sunday off in 3, the enthusiasm of the men who voluntarily paraded, drilled and trained twice a week and on their free Sunday mornings is obvious. Production of aircraft and aircraft parts was of vital importance and all ranks were often called upon to work night and day, but the attendance at all parades was always good and the keenness of all ranks never wavered.

In November 1941 Capt. E. Mack, M.C., Cheshire Regiment, was appointed Adjutant and Quartermaster to the Battalion with effect from 24th November 1941 and thanks to his initiative and hard working ability an efficient military organisation was brought into being.

The first Battalion Orders were issued on 1st December 1941 and at the organisation of the Battalion on 1st January was as follows :

Battalion Headquarters
South Marston Factory
Commanding Officer :
Lt.-Col. M. Ormonde Darby, O.B.E.
Second in Command :
Maj. P. L. Holmes, D.S.C.
Adjutant & Quartermaster :
Capt. E. Mack, M.C.
Medical Officer : Lt. D. S. Patton
Signalling Officer : 2/Lt. Griffiths

Home Guard Detachment, The Close
Assistant Adjutant: Capt. S. C. Bushell
Assistant Quartermaster: Lt. Thompson
Platoon Commander :
Lt. W. Boughton-Fox

" B " Company
Company Headquarters :
South Marston Factory
Company Commander : Maj. McKecnie
Platoon Commanders : Lt. Tipper, Lt. Miles, Lt. Hamilton, Lt. Bolton.

" C " Company
Company Headquarters :
24 Shop, G.W.R. Works
Company Commander :
Capt. H. C. Hill
Platoon Commanders : Lt. W. E. M. Miller, Lt. A. A. Bartlett.

" D " Company
Company Headquarters :
Sevenhampton Factory

Company Commander :
Capt. M. C. Holmes
Platoon Commander :
Lt. J. C. Hilderbrands

" E ' Company
Company Headquarters :
Blunsdon Factory
Administration Officer : Lt. Ferry
Platoon Commander :
Lt. Main, D.C.M., M.M.

" F " Company
Company Headquarters :
Flight Sheds, 2
Company Commander :
Capt. E. Morton
Platoon Commanders : 2/Lt. Patience, 2/Lt. A. L. Smith.

" G " Company
Company Headquarters :
Pleasey's Factory
Company Commander :
Capt. R. D. Bibby
Platoon Commanders : Lt. W. Christie, 2/Lt. G. W. E. Knowles.

" H " Company
Company Headquarters :
24 Shop, G.W.R. Works
Acting Company Commander :
Lt. G. T. Firth
Temporarily Unattached : Capt. Whyte and Capt. Boby.

1942
A year of steady training and increasing efficiency in the face of the difficulties of long working hours and the ebb and flow of personnel due to production and service requirements.

In January of this year meetings of company commanders were inaugarated, and certificates in appreciation of good service were awarded to C.S.M. C. M. Hancock and Sgt. J. Neale in the New Year's Honours List.

The strength of the Battalion was gradually increasing and during March platoons were organised into battle squads and as platoons reached establishment additional platoons were commenced.

Training in battle drill and battle craft took place and the various companies saw their first training film.

The H.Q. Detachment of 1941 was now incorporated into " F " Company. Further slight changes in organisation were made in April when " E " Company was incorporated with " C " Company and the personnel at Bellman Hanger were attached to " B " Company. Personnel at the County Road Stores were also incorporated into " C " Company.

Demonstrations of unarmed combat throughout the Battalion added another interesting item to the training programme.

On the 17th May the Area Commander visited the Battalion and saw companies at training.

An Army Council Instruction published during this month laid down a standard of efficiency for the Home Guard, a standard of efficiency which the Battalion individually and collectively set out to attain. In addition to the usual training a number of lectures were given during the month of June, one to officers by the Sub-area Commander, another also to officers on " The Rôle of the Home Guard " by officers of the Home Guard School of Instruction, Bulford, and one to all ranks by Lt. Lashman on " Lessons from Crete ".

Maj. P. L. Holmes, D.S.C., took over command of " D " Company and Capt. A. P. Whyte was appointed Intelligence Officer.

Battalion Orders in July cited the award of Certificates in Appreciation of Good Service in the King's Birthday Honours List to C.S.M. Peirce and Sgt. Bullock.

The Group Commander Wiltshire Home Guard inspected " B " Company during September and in October an H.Q. Company of specialist sub-units was formed.

During the month of November a visit by the Headquarter Travelling Wing to the area was taken advantage of by as many officers and N.C.O.s as possible, although the prior claim of production caused disappointment to many others, but the knowledge gained was passed on to the benefit of all. In December Maj. D. McKechnie was transferred to the A.A. and Maj. R. D. Bibby took over command of " B " Company. The formation of an A.A. battery " Z " equipment in Swindon drained the Battalion of a number of good men but recruiting went on and the gaps were filled.

1943

It is considered that during this year the Home Guard reached the peak of its existence, the personnel were becomming well trained, P.S.I.s had been posted to every battalion for training and assisting the Adjutant, and A. & Q. officers had also been posted for their special duties, and every three or four battalions had a training officer to assist each battalion commander in the training of his battalion. In addition to the above all Home Guard battalions were now very well equipped and armed with many and various weapons such as Smith Guns, spigot mortars,

Northovers and anti-tank guns, and lastly, but most important of all, there were factory canteens available for training purposes and in this area particularly the battalions were very fortunate in having access to rifle ranges, and bombing ranges, in close proximity to Swindon.

Another visit from the Headquarters Travelling Wing and Travelling Cinema was of great benefit to training and further Certificates in Appreciation of Good Service were awarded in the New Year's Honours List to Maj. D. G. McKechnie, Sgt. (now 2/Lt.) G. G. Giles and Corp. (now 2/Lt.) W. Baker.

In February Capt. A. Hails, R.A. was appointed Quartermaster and Administrative Officer to the Battalion and Sgt. (now 2/Lt.) Cookson was appointed i/c Intelligence.

Early in March a 30 yards range for the use of the Battalion was completed and opened at the South Marston Factory. During this month the Battalion lost the services of Capt. E. J. H. F. Moreton who relinquished his appointment and the command of " F " Company was assumed by Lt. A. J. Edwards.

Capt. J. W. Clough was transferred from " B " to " A " Company in April, assuming command, and in addition becoming Signals Officer, whilst Capt. F. F. Foord relinquished command of " A " Company and became Second in Command " B " Company.

The third anniversary of the formation of the Home Guard was celebrated throughout the country by special parades on Sunday 16th May. In Swindon a march past of the local units was held. Taking part were the 5th, 9th, 11th, 13th Battalions and the 101st A.A. Troop, Wiltshire Regiment Home Guard.

This was the first time the Battalion had paraded as a unit and the general public had, for the first time, the opportunity of seeing all the local units on parade. Big crowds lined the streets and the parade created a good impression. Lt. T. B. Jones from the 9th Battalion assumed command of " H " Company during the month.

In June the following extract from the *London Gazette* dated 23rd May 1943 was published in Battalion Orders :

" To be Additional Member of the Military Division of the Most Excellent Order of the British Empire : Capt. G. T. Firth."

Week-end camps were held during June, July and August and proved a welcome change in training.

Capt. J. W. Clough was promoted Maj. and to be Second in Command, whilst Lt. Young assumed command of " E " Company.

Authority was received during July for the employment of women to assist the Home Guard and the necessary establishment was rapidly filled.

This month also, saw the assembling of the first Board of Examiners for Proficiency Tests.

" D " Company submitted the first quota of candidates for examination.

In addition to the week-end camps the use of the bombing range at Coleshill was obtained during August for the many candidates for Proficiency Tests.

Lt.-Col. B. A. M. Hall, O.B.E., R.A. (retired) assumed command of the Battalion on 3rd September 1943 vice Lt.-Col. M. Ormonde-Darby, O.B.E. who left the district.

During this month the Battalion took part in its first large scale exercise, the " White Horse " Exercise, in conjunction with other units in the area and with the co-operation of strong forces of American troops. The Battalion Headquarters was removed from South Marston Factory to the Old National Schools, Stratton St. Margaret.

October brought a return visit of the Travelling Wing and Lt. (A/Capt.) W. E. M. Miller was appointed Weapons Training Officer.

Examinations for Proficiency Tests were continued and central training in weapons, signals, intelligence and first aid was instituted. During November light A.A. troops were formed at the various factories.

Under company arrangements plans were made for the entertainment of the wives and children of personnel during Christmas and the early part of the New Year, plans that were all successfully carried out, and another year was past.

1944

During the early months of the year instructions were received that the A.A. rôle was the primary rôle of the Home Guard and that all other training was to be subordinated to this. In consequence a new nomenclature of companies came into existance as follows :

" B " Company at South Marston Factory became " A " Troop and manned 6 Hispano's 20 m.m. guns for A.A. defence.

" F " Company at F.S.2. became " B " Troop and manned 4 Hispano's 20 m.m. guns for A.A. defence.

" E " Company at Blunsdon became " C " Troop and manned 4 Browning's ·303s for A.A. defence.

During the year visits were paid to Sandbanks near Bournemouth and Portishead for practice against towed targets.

The responsibilities for training and maintenance and cleanliness of equipment of the L.A.A. troops were taken over by the A.A. Regiment in this area who provided the necessary instructions and personnel for this purpose.

During the month of March an interesting exercise " Stirling " was carried out with the U.S. troops in the vicinity who acted as paratroops for the attack on South Marston.

During the month of May a ceremonial Parade was held in Swindon for the fourth anniversary of the formation of the Home Guard, in which the Battalion took part, and they marched through the streets of Swindon with 2 of the 4 anti-tank 2-pounder guns which had recently been issued to the Battalion.

Changes of Personnel in the Battalion

The strength of the Battalion up to 1943 had been about 1,200 men, but during the year 1944 a great reduction of roughly 50 per cent in the personnel took place owing to Armstrong Whitworth's contract for supplying Stirlings being terminated and most of the Home Guard belonging to this Battalion were distributed over various parts of England. The loss of so many trained men, especially specialist, inflicted a severe blow on the Battalion and many useful officers' services were among the members dispersed.

" Salute the Soldier " Week

Fifty men of "H" Company took part in a ceremonial parade in Swindon during July for the inauguration of this War Savings Week.

Role During Invasion

During the period of the invasion of the Continent by the Second Army and the Canadian Army the Home Guard took on various responsibilities from 6th June ("D" Day) and all factory guards were mounted and Battalion Headquarters manned day and night.

Early in September the military situation was so promising that all V.P. guards were dismounted and all duties, parades, etc., were put on a voluntary basis. The whole question of the "Standing Down" of the Home Guard at an early date was carefully considered and plans made.

The date of the "Stand Down" of the Home Guard was decided by His Majesty the King to be Sunday 3rd December, 1944, at which farewell parades would be held all over the country, as decided by battalion commanders.

In this Battalion three privates were sent to London for the Home Guard parade there, at which His Majesty the King took the salute. In Swindon the 5th, 11th and 13th Battalions of the Home Guard took part in a ceremonial march through the streets of Swindon and the salute was taken by Maj.-Gen. R. L. Laurie, C.B., C.B.E., Commander, Salisbury Plain District, who afterwards addressed the troops in the 5th Battalion Drill Hall.

During the month of November a very outstanding rifle competition was held between "H" Company of this Battalion and "C" Company of the 3rd Gloucestershire Battalion Home Guard on the rifle range at Liddington, at which "H" Company of this Battalion won.

On 23rd November a very successful supper and smoking concert was held in the Southbrook Hall, Swindon at which some 300 members of the Home Guard, their wives and friends sat down to a supper followed by a smoking concert. Those in attendance were the Mayor and Mayoress of Swindon ; Col. Fitzgerald, Commander, North East Sector ; Col. Darby late Commander of the 11th Wiltshire Battalion Home Guard ; Mr. Woodley, Vickers Armstrong, and Mr. Shepherd of Armstrong Whitworth Aircraft Ltd.

Col. Hall, Commander of the Battalion, presented Capt. Mack, Adjutant with a cigarette case, and a flask and cuff-links to Capt. Hails, A. & Q. Officer in appreciation of their services with the Battalion for which they had served during the past two or three years.

12TH BATTALION WILTSHIRE HOME GUARD

THE formation of the Battalion commenced in January 1943, from employees of the B.A.C. and B.S.A. factories at Hawthorn. The Battalion was numbered the 12th and allotted a ceiling strength of 1,000.

During that month Lt. E. C. Baker and 77 other ranks were posted from " K " Company of the 1st Battalion Wiltshire Home Guard, and in this way the foundation was laid.

Maj. C. H. Tucker, the Business Manager of the B.A.C. assumed command of the Battalion and on 1st June 1943, was promoted to the rank of Lt.-Col.

The strength mounted slowly, mostly by postings in from other units, the men having been transferred to the staff of the B.A.C.

In February 1943, the Commanding Officer directed that no promotions or appointments, either to commissioned or non-commissioned rank, would be made except from personnel who had passed through a cadre course and obtained a satisfactory report.

The first cadre class was run during February and March 1943, with very satisfactory results, and the students were promoted and filled appointments to which they were best suited.

The permanent staff arrived in the middle of February 1943, and consisted of Adjutant (Capt. A. Shipp), Capt. A. & Q. Duties (Capt. R. Jones) and P.S.I. (Sgt. A. Weston).

Cadre classes were continued, and the training of potential officers and N.C.O.s retained priority so that a sound framework could be constructed to ensure that the training of the Battalion could be carried out with a sufficient number of efficient instructors. Weapon training being always regarded as of paramount importance.

In March 1943, the strength had risen sufficiently to form up into three weak companies, H.Q. which consisted solely of specialists, " A " Company, all of whom resided at Corsham, and " B " Company who were located in Thorny Pits and other hostel sites. At this time 2/Lt. Brooks (Intelligence Officer) assumed command of H.Q. Company, " A " Company was commanded by Capt. W. A. Rushton (who had been posted in from another Home Guard unit) and the " B " Company Commander was 2/Lt. H. Westcott. For tactical work " A " and " B " Companies both came under the command of Officer Commanding " A " Company.

On 1st April 1943, 2/Lt. H. Westcott resigned his commission through ill-health and the command of " B " Company was taken over by the Second in Command, Maj. E. C. Baker, until the arrival of Maj. W. E. Cowan Dickie, who was posted in and accepted in the rank of major, and this officer then assumed command of " B " Company.

During June 1943, Capt. R. Jones (Quartermaster) left the Battalion owing to ill-health. This left the unit without a quartermaster until 15th December 1943, when Capt. H. Marshall filled this appointment.

The question of the defence of the entrances of the factory above ground was now fully covered by " A " and " B " Companies and the defence of the factory below ground was solved on the 10th June 1943, by the formation of another company which was named " D " Company. This company was composed entirely of the factory police who were nearly all ex-service personnel, and command of the company was taken over by the Police Superintendent, Superintendent H. C. Hill, who was appointed in the rank of major. The defence of the factory, both above and below ground, was now shaped, and as the strength increased, was tightened up. Sub-artillery and light automatic weapons were drawn, personnel were trained, and weapons sited.

In December 1943, the Commanding Officer decided on a reorganisation of the Battalion, chiefly with a view to placing all the defended localities above ground under one command, and the situation on the completion was that H.Q. Company became " A " Company, and was comprised of No. 1 Platoon (Signals), No. 2 Platoon (Intelligence), No. 3 Platoon (Pioneers), No. 4 Platoon (Administration) and Nos. 5 and 6 Mobile Battle Platoons. Officer Commanding " A " Company, Capt. L. Glasscoe.

" B " Company under the command of Maj. W. A. Rushton, consisted of 7, 8, 9, 10, 11, and 12 Battle Platoons, and No. 13 Platoon which controlled all sub-artillery weapons. " D " Company was renamed " C " Company and contained Nos. 14 and 15 Platoons.

The reorganisation left Maj. W. E. Cowan Dickie supernumerary to establishment and his commission was relinquished.

The Battalion continued through 1944 to carry out a progressive training programme, culminating in a series of attacks by the mobile platoons of " A " Company attacking all D.L.s in turn, to show up any weaknesses.

The strength in August 1944 had mounted to 732, and " A " and " B " Companies both with a strength of over 300, were becoming unweildy. The Commanding Officer then decided to expand to Battalion Headquarters H.Q. Company, three rifle companies and a support company to allow for more flexibility and to allow other promising officers to have a command.

This assumed shape during September and on receipt of the instructions regarding termination of compulsory parades the Battalion situation was :

Battalion Headquarters which included Intelligence personnel.

H.Q. Company : No. 1 Platoon (Signals), No. 2 Platoon (Medical), No. 3 Platoon (Administration). Officer Commanding Company, Capt. L. Glasscoe.

" *A* " (*Rifle Company*) : 4, 5 and 6 Platoons. Officer Commanding, Maj. W. A. Rushton

" *B* " *Rifle Company*) : 7, 8 and 9 Platoons. Officer Commanding, Capt. E. W. Roberts.

" C " (*Police Company*) : 10 and 11 Platoons. Officer Commanding, Maj. H. C. Hill.

" D " (*Support Company*) : 12, 13 and 14 (Sub-artillery Platoons), 15 (Machine-gun Platoon) and 16 (Mobile Platoon). Officer Commanding Company, Capt. M. H. Prigg.

On the information that sub-artillery was being withdrawn a slight modification of " D " Company was made—12, 13 and 14 Platoons were reformed to 12 and 13 Battle Platoons. The Machine-gun Platoon became No. 14 Platoon and the Mobile Platoon became No. 15.

On the formation of Sector Headquarters the Battalion trained and provided the whole of the Western Sector Signals and Intelligence personnel. These manned and controlled the Western Sector Headquarters under command of Col. A. H. Burn during garrison and other exercises and received highly satisfactory reports. The Signal Office was organised by Lt. S. Lees and the Intelligence Office by Lt. D. Laurie.

The Battalion on the whole although only an " infant " was thriving and the skill at arms displayed by a great number of the personnel was of a very high order.

13TH BATTALION WILTSHIRE HOME GUARD

CREATED from a nucleus of 17 officers and 623 other ranks of " F " Company, 5th Battalion Wiltshire Home Guard, the 13th Battalion (G.W.R.) Wiltshire Home Guard was formed on 1st May 1943, and placed under the command of Lt.-Col. S. A. Dyer, who had, since June 1940, been Company Commander of the parent company.

The original company had been recruited exclusively from amongst employees of the Great Western Railway Company in Swindon with, as its primary object, the defence of the G.W.R. Works against enemy attack and sabotage. Their operational rôle was naturally somewhat limited but as the lengthy perimeter of the works, railway station and yards was to a large extent the north and west perimeter of the town, and a key point in its defence from the north-west, it was possible to embody them without difficulty into the general town scheme.

With changing circumstances and increased commitments it became necessary to expand beyond " company " strength, without in any way destroying its place in the Sector scheme or its identification with the Railway Company.

Even prior to the formation of the Battalion it was found that the Company Headquarters which had served for more than two and a half years were inadequate and the G.W.R. Company had placed a portion of No. 3 Emlyn Square at the disposal of the Home Guard, free of cost.

Upon the formation of the Battalion these premises were taken over in their entirety, and put into habitable condition, again free of cost, so some initial difficulties were solved very quickly and the newly formed Battalion was able to commence functioning forthwith.

Whilst within the limited scope of these notes it is only desired to deal with the 13th Battalion as such, some brief reference to its early days as a company of the 5th Battalion is necessary in order to obtain a true perspective.

Immediately following Mr. Anthony Eden's broadcast on 14th May 1940, it was evident that many hundreds of men were ready to respond and, in fact, did so by reporting to the police stations in Swindon the following day. The G.W.R. Company realising the vital necessity of safeguarding the lines of communication, issued an appeal for the formation of railway units whose primary function, within the general scheme, would be the defence of railway bridges, signal boxes, junctions, lines, works and places of vital importance to traffic. It was natural that railway employees would be far more familiar with the layout of such places than any one else and it was therefore to such men the Railway Company looked for assistance. The response was immediate and almost overwhelming, and more than 500 men attended a meeting in the G.W.R. Mess-room in London Street on the 3rd June to hear an outline of the scheme by Mr. J. Auld, then Principal Assistant to the Chief Mechanical Engineer.

The first five members signed Enrolment Forms W.3066 on the 30th May 1940 and on the 1st June the patrolling of railway premises commenced. Organisation for the enrolment of the remainder of the volunteers was immediately set up, but it was quickly found that to retain in the G.W.R. Local Defence Volunteer Company the whole of their employees who were anxious to serve therein would have a detrimental effect in the formation of other companies. As a result, in response to a request from the late Lt.-Col. B. L. Birley, D.S.O., who was in command of the Local Defence Volunteers for the area, volunteers were called for to transfer to other companies, mainly in the vicinity of the men's homes. This ensured general " levelling " of strength throughout the various companies, but it should be recorded that after the first few days during which the number of volunteers was decided purely by the capacity to enrol them, the strength of the G.W.R. Company never fell below 450 and notwithstanding the increasing strain thrown on men by longer hours of work, and the many hundreds of men who were either directed away from Swindon by the Ministry of Labour to work elsewhere, the constant wastage due to call-up for the Forces, physical incapacity, etc., the Company had a strength, as previously mentioned, of 640 officers and men when it became the 13th Battalion.

Personnel

At the stand down of the Battalion, the chain of command, and strength, was as given below :

Battalion Commanding Officer :
Lt.-Col. S. A. Dyer
Second in Command :
Maj. H. J. Morse
Intelligence Officer : Lt. R. Fricker
Medical Officer : Maj. A. W. C. Bennett
Junior Liaison Officer :
Lt. R. Bromley
Signals Officer : 2/Lt. S. V. Satchell
Adjutant :
Capt. J. A. Haynes (K.O.R.R.)
Welfare and Messing Officer :
Lt. W. E. Miller
Gas Officer : Lt. M. A. E. Tucker
Quartermaster :
Capt. T. H. Tarry (R.I.R.)
Ammunition Officer : Lt. W. G. Clack
Press Liaison Officer and Assistant Adjutant : Lt. E. A. H. Chegwidden

P.S.I's: C.S.M. Lavington (K.O.R.R.), C.S.M. Biddle (Hampshire Regt.)
Motor Transport Officer : Lt. F. Raven
Weapon Training Officer :
Lt. H. W. Tompkins
R.S.M. : A. G. Head
Armourer : Sgt. G. Dibsdall
Battalion Medical Orderly :
Sgt. S. W. Gullis
R.Q.M.S. : W. H. Boucher
Provost Sergeant :
Sgt. F. J. Wright, D.C.M.
Orderly Room Sergeant :
Col.-Sgt. W. H. Day
" A " *Company :* Maj. F. I. V. Day, Capt. T. L. Whipp
" B " *Company :* Maj. A. G. Porter, Capt. R. Purbick

143

" C " Company : Maj. F. Coombs, Capt. A. Wright	*" E " Company :* Maj. F. Dance, Capt. J. L. Roberts
" D " Company : Maj. J. Brooks, Capt. W. Batchelor, D.C.M.	*L.A.A. Troop :* Capt. A. L. C. Young

Total strength of Battalion : 981.

It will be realised that to function as a complete entity at Battalion level is very different from being a company and consequently training, administrative and " Q " branches are on a much larger scale and scope.

The first step necessary in the building up of the Battalion was the selection and appointment of Regular Army officers as Adjutant and Quartermaster (A. & Q.) respectively, and on the 26th May 1940, Capt. E. W. Thomas (Pioneer Corps) was attached to the 13th Battalion for A. & Q. duties, followed on the 9th July by Capt. J. A. Haynes (King's Own) as Adjutant.

From this time rapid strides were made in the reorganisation of the whole structure. It had been built on sound foundations but needed a tremendous expenditure of time, ability and energy on the part of the Commanding Officer and Adjutant to overcome its " growing pains " as it emerged from its chrysalis state.

To evolve companies from the previous platoons was a fairly simple task although needing some expansion of administrative personnel, and this was quickly dealt with, the order of precedence being decided by the seniority of the then platoon commanders. One of the next problems was the appointment of the various " specialist " officers necessary in a battalion, and having secured these, to build up effective sections able fully to carry out their respective functions. In view of the fact that Home Guard duties were performed in " spare " time, consideration had to be given not only to the qualifications of officers for their particular posts but to their availability.

Gradually all difficulties were surmounted and in a few months specially trained officers had been appointed to cover the following duties, and the sections were smoothly functioning :

> Medical Officer
> Signals Officer
> Intelligence Officer
> Gas Officer
> Weapons Training Officer
> Ammunition Officer
> Press Liaison Officer and Assistant Adjutant
> Transport Officer
> Welfare and Messing Officer

Later, a further section was formed specifically for the defence of the works against low flying aircraft. This was known as the L.A.A. Section, and was founded on a somewhat different footing from the other sections as the operation and training was through A.A. Command although its administration was through the Battalion Headquarters to S.P.D. The personnel of 3 officers (1 captain and 2 lieutenants) and 100 other ranks was recruited from the 13th Battalion.

Properly to deal with each section would require a history of each but such is not the present object.

Weapons and Equipment

As is now well known, when the Local Defence Volunteer force was formed, equipment was nil and weapons negligible ; being confined to a few assorted rifles. The gradual issue of equipment and weapons began before the Local Defence Volunteers became the Home Guard and whilst the 13th Battalion was still a part of the 5th Battalion, and its history has no place in this record, though much could be written of the change from home made cudgels to machine-guns. In the case of the 13th Battalion there is, therefore, no such dramatic variation in weapons and weapon strength as in Battalions formed earlier, but the following comparisons may be of some interest :

	On Formation 1 May 1943	On " Stand Down " 1 Nov. 1944
Rifles, ·300	250	250
,, ·22	4	17
,, E.Y.	7	39
,, L.A. Browning	1	1
Guns, Browning	1	4
,, Lewis	4	11
,, Vickers	–	5
Northover Projectors	3	3
Spigot Mortars	4	8
Smith Guns	4	8
Guns, 2-pounder anti-tank	–	8
Carbines, Sten	350	677
Pistols, Signal	–	2
		L.A.A.
Guns, 20 m.m. Hispano	–	9

With the exception of the Sten Guns, signal pistols and E.Y. rifles, the whole of these additional arms were received during 1944 and as, in the case of the Vickers, the 2-pounder anti-tank and the 20 m.m. Hispano guns, it was new equipment to the Home Guard, some intensive training was necessary thoroughly to understand and master the technique.

Equipment, too, has been markedly increased as the training of the various sections has developed, but perhaps the only item of general interest was the supply of " walkie-talkie " wireless sets by means of which members of the Signal Section could transmit and receive messages through portable sets strapped to them.

Camps

The first Battalion camp was held at Castle Eaton in August 1943 within a few months of formation and in view of this it was thought advisable to confine it to about 100 selected members—mainly with the idea of combining the camp with a junior leaders' course. Capt. J. A. Haynes (Adjutant) and Capt. E. W. Thomas (Quartermaster), undertook responsibility for the whole camp and it proved to be an unqualified success. With the assistance of the Chief Instructor N.E. Sector (Lt.-Col. Broom, D.S.O., M.C.) the officers, N.C.O.s and men went through a week of intensive training, both theoretical and practical, which covered physical training, lectures, demonstrations, fire control, battle drill, messages—verbal and written, recce. patrols, fieldcraft and night operations.

Experience so gained was put to good use during the winter training and the following year (1944) it was arranged to hold " company " camps for the Battalion. This was necessary not only by reason of the number of men wishing to participate (over 300), which would have made individual instruction difficult, but also to avoid the absence from work of too many men at the same time. This also gave company commanders an excellent opportunity of exercising their men under appropriate conditions.

These camps covered a period of three weeks, " B " and " E " Companies taking the first, followed by " C " and " D " and finally " A " Company had the third week. During the whole of the time Capt. J. A. Haynes (Adjutant) and Capt. T. H. Tarry (Quartermaster) took control in looking after the training programme, feeding and accommodation and the complete success of the venture was in large measure due to their efforts. Maj. J. E. B. Stewart, the N.E. Sector Training Officer spent a good deal of time at the camp and his instruction and advice was greatly appreciated.

A rather more ambitious programme was carried out than in the first camp and the training covered theoretical and practical work on rifle, grenade, Sten Gun, machine-guns, 2-pounder anti-tank gun, Smith Gun, spigot mortar, T.O.E.T., application of fire, battlecraft, individual stalk, crossing obstacles, field signals, selection of lines of advance, squad and platoon battle drill, tactical battle drill, patrols, platoon in attack, house clearing and a night scheme. The final period for all companies was devoted to battle innoculation at Ogbourne.

Mixed with the training there was a sports and visitors' day each week, and as a final wind up to the series of camps, Lt.-Col. S. A. Dyer arranged an officers' conference, when the Battalion officers met for the evening and had as their guests Col. W. F. Beach of the U.S. Army and Lt.-Col. A. E. Beswick of the 5th Battalion Home Guard.

It was during the week when " C " and " D " Companies were at camp that the Sector Commander, Col. F. W. Wilson FitzGerald, D.S.O., M.C., and Col. K. W. C. Grand, the Railway Liaison Officer, visited the camp and presented Certificates for Good Service that had been awarded to W.O. 1 (R.S.M.) A. G. Head and Sgt. S. W. Gullis.

Special Parades

The first special parade of the 13th Battalion after formation was a drumhead Service held at the County Ground on Sunday, 6th June 1943. The service, conducted by the Rev. L. A. Erett, C.F., then Vicar of St. Augustines, was followed by an inspection by Lt.-Col. Dyer of the five companies and the special sections of signallers, cyclists, ambulance, static and mobile weapons, during the course of which a demonstration was given by four teams operating Smith Guns. Col. Dyer was accompanied by Mr. K. W. C. Grand (Assistant General Manager, G.W.R. —now also Railway Liaison Officer), Mr. F. W. Hawksworth (Chief Mechanical Engineer, G.W.R. Company) and Lt.-Col. A. E. Beswick, Officer Commanding 5th Battalion Wiltshire Home Guard.

Under the heading of special parades should also be included the Battalion rifle meeting at Liddington on 5th September 1943. There was a representative gathering of more than 130 all ranks and the events included shooting for a company cup, platoon shield and an individual cup ; in addition there was a " pool bull " competition. Winners of the events on this occasion were :

Company Cup   " E " Company
Platoon Shield   Signals Platoon, H.Q. Company
Individual Cup   Sgt. E. G. Tucker, " A " Company

Mr. F. W. Hawksworth, J.P., the G.W.R. Company's Chief Mechanical Engineer was an interested spectator and presented the trophies.

Remembrance Day, 1943, was commemorated by a Battalion Parade and attendance at St. Mark's Church for Divine Service, during which the lessons were read by Capt. F. J. Dance, Officer Commanding " E " Company. After the service the Battalion marched to the Cenotaph.

On the 16th April 1944 the Battalion held a parade on the Rodbourne Recreation Ground when Col. F. W. Wilson FitzGerald, D.S.O., M.C., Sector Commander, presented a Certificate of Good Service awarded in conjunction with the New Year's Honours List, to Col.-Sgt. (C.Q.M.S.) R. E. S. Wheeler, " B " Company, and afterwards inspected the Battalion. This was the first public appearance of the Battalion band.

The second Battalion rifle meeting took place in September 1944 and once more the contests for the various trophies were very keen. This time " A " Company had an extremely good day and nearly carried off all the honours, the results being :

Company Cup   " A " Company
Platoon Shield   No. 1 Platoon, " A " Company
Individual Cup   Lt. F. Webber, " E " Company

As on the previous occasion Mr. F. W. Hawksworth, J.P. and other officials of the G.W.R. Company attended and witnessed some of the events, as also did the Sector Commander, Col. F. W. Wilson FitzGerald, D.S.O., M.C. Afterwards Mr. Hawksworth presented the trophies.

On the Sunday morning following the announcement that in future the Home Guard would revert to a voluntary organisation, the 13th Battalion held a special parade and more than 400 members attended. The new conditions were outlined by Lt.-Col. Dyer and there was a practically unanimous wish expressed that the Battalion should continue to function on the basis of a parade for training, etc., each Sunday morning and that was carried out right up to the date of " Stand Down ".

Since its formation the Battalion has participated in the public parades held on such occasions as the Home Guard Anniversaries, Remembrance Days, and " Salute the Soldier " weeks.

The last time the Battalion paraded was for Remembrance Sunday when they attended St. Augustine's Church and the Battalion band participated in the service by playing for some of the hymns. The Rev. James Evans, Vicar of St. Augustines gave the address.

Instructional Courses

The Battalion sent 103 officers and other ranks on different courses of instruction to places ranging from Plymouth to Yorkshire and had no failures. Results generally were excellent and no less than 7 members secured " A " Certificates. At the time of " Stand Down " there were fully qualified instructors in every branch of Home Guard work, including 9 in chemical warfare.

General

The Battalion had, in addition to its actual strength, 115 men held on supernumerary strength, who had been enrolled into the 220th (101st) Wiltshire Rocket Battery, but for whom the 13th was the parent Battalion. In March 1944 arrangements were made to withdraw certain men from the Battalion for transfer to the Rocket Battery and, after considering hours of duty and physical fitness for the particular work required of them, 25 men were so transferred.

Originally the Battalion ceiling was fixed at 1,200 and taking into account the 115 men held on Supernumerary strength this had practically been attained.

Endeavour had always been made to create and foster a recreational and social side in conjunction with the normal activities of the Battalion, and this proved very satisfactory. Numerous functions were held by the Battalion and the various companies ranging from miniature rifle competitions to dances, whist drives, skittle and snooker matches, concerts, etc., and this no doubt contributed towards the spirit of comradeship which existed throughout.

During the " Salute the Soldier " Week in July 1944, the Battalion raised no less than £2,322-5-6 although its original target was only £750.

Donations and subscriptions have been made to many deserving cases such as the British Red Cross Society.

It is worthy of mention that four members of the Battalion now hold Certificates for Good Service, three have previously been mentioned in this report and the fourth is Lt. C. W. Leader, " E " Company (granted when C.S.M. of " F " Company, 5th Battalion).

One member of the Battalion—Pte. J. P. Osbourne—saved a woman from drowning in a lake about 50 feet deep by diving in fully clothed, bringing her to the side and subsequently applying artificial respiration. Notification of this act duly appeared in the Battalion Orders.

220TH (101ST WILTSHIRE HOME GUARD) ROCKET A.A. BATTERY

History of Formation and Service

FOLLOWING the decision to form a rocket A.A. battery for the A.A. defence of Swindon, a meeting of employers and trade union officials was held at the Town Hall and the general scheme and manpower requirements explained by Brig. Morley of 64th A.A. Brigade. The Battery was, with similar batteries sited at Oxford and Gloucester, to form the 20th A.A. Regiment. Maj. D. G. McKechnie, Home Guard, was appointed Home Guard Battery Commander. The Ministry of Labour undertook to provide the necessary manpower and recruiting started in September 1942, temporary headquarters being obtained at Church Place, Swindon, where the newly formed Regular component under Maj. H. Jarvis, R.A. was established. After a short stay at Church Place, Battery Headquarters was moved to Stratton and the Drill Hall, Prospect, Swindon was taken for training, which consisted of a three weeks' intensive course, covering basic, projector drill, ballistics and gas.

It was obvious from the first that unsuitable men were being enrolled and the attention of the Ministry of Labour was called to this but the Ministry had been advised that " shift workers " were suitable for " Z " batteries and no action was taken to " vet " men prior to enrolment. This short-sighted policy caused endless trouble when the Battery commenced operational duty. After three batches of recruits had been trained the first 8 officers and 20 N.C.O.s were selected and these were reinforced by 4 officers who transferred from the 9th Battalion Wiltshire Home Guard with 80 men of the Lower Stratton Platoon. These candidates were given a special course of " Z " gunnery and this policy of selecting candidates for commissions and requiring them to take an officer cadet course has been adhered to throughout the life of the Battery with good results. After approximately 800 men had been trained the Battery commenced operational duty in April 1943, with officers and N.C.O.s doing duty on one night in six and privates on one night in eight. The presence of unsuitable men was felt immediately, the absenteeism being appalling, reaching as high a figure as 50–60 per cent mainly through shift work although a fair amount of avoidable absence was apparent. The effort to combat this state of affairs was weak and ineffective and the trouble persisted.

In June 1943, the Battery received a severe blow in the loss of Maj. H. Jarvis, R.A. Maj. Jarvis had the complete confidence of all ranks and his departure was deeply felt by all ranks. Maj. Jarvis was replaced by Maj. J. W. Watson, M.C., R.A. Maj. McKechnie, Home Guard, also left the Battery on joining the Royal Navy. Capt. S. J. Harris, Home Guard was promoted major and took command of the Battery. Further Home Guard officers and N.C.O.s were appointed and the strength was now sufficient to place the Battery on a complete relief basis, the following officers being appointed to command reliefs.

" A " Capt. J. Phipps, Home Guard   " E " Capt. R. Hammond, Home Guard
" B " Capt. W. Scribbins, Home Guard   " F " Capt. A. Joynes, Home Guard
" C " Capt. G. Staniforth, Home Guard   " G " Capt. C. Duff, Home Guard
" D " Capt. W. Beardmore, Home Guard   " H " Lt. P. Raymond, Home Guard

The absentee question was now tackled very seriously and following many reports and requests from the Battery Commander, a conference was held at Stratton under the direction of Maj.-Gen. Curtis, G.O.C. Salisbury Plain District. At this conference the Officer Commanding 5th Wiltshire Home Guard was ordered to transfer 200 men immediately and a further 200 within three months. The Battery Commander ordered a strict vetting of all new entrants to the Battery.

A complete survey of the Battery was made and all unsuitable men transferred to G.S. battalions. The manpower position was now prominently before all concerned and the appointment of Maj.-Gen. E. O. Lewin, C.B., C.M.G., D.S.O. made a tremendous difference in the effort to get this problem solved. Manpower Boards were set up and with Gen. Lewin's great experience and influence the position steadily improved. Very considerable assistance was also given by Col. K. W. C. Grand, Railway Liaison Officer, who was whole-heartedly behind the Battery.

Great strides were now being made towards increased operational efficiency, every officer qualifying as a plotting officer, 5 passing out as T.C.O.s and others were about to take the course when the Regiment was transferred to 46th Brigade whose policy did not encourage Home Guard T.C.O.s. Twelve officers passed the G.L. Course and the standard attained was exceedingly high. The Home Guard officer strength was still further improved and the policy of giving the utmost encouragement to men transferring from the G.S. battalions paid a high dividend, no fewer than 16 passing the necessary courses and qualifying as commissioned officers.

The Adjutant, Capt. A. St. J. Sibborn, R.A. was replaced by Capt. H. D. P. Drew, R.A., a capable and energetic officer whose work cannot be too highly praised. A further change was made in the R.A. command, Maj. Watson being replaced by Maj. J. T. Hetzel, R.A.

The manpower position still caused anxiety but the definite policy which had been laid down that no unsuitable man should be enrolled was maintained, and although this caused a certain amount of criticism in various quarters it became obvious the policy was correct and the following comparison completely justifies the system of vetting employed.

	Men on Strength	Absenteeism	Projectors manned
June 1943	1,500	50 = 60%	22
Sept. 1944	1,200	10 = 15%*	50

*=less than 2% avoidable.

Numerous " stand to's " were dealt with but the Battery did not get an opportunity to fire, as the only time a target came within range friendly aircraft were in the air over the site. Two officers proved unsatisfactory and were discharged and several good officers had to resign owing to leaving the district. Prominent among these was Capt. Duff whose fine work was much appreciated. Capt. Duff's relief was taken over by Capt. R. Henderson who proved very satisfactory. Lt. Raymond left the Battery through ill health and " H " Relief was taken over by Capt. J. Barnes, M.M., an experienced officer who fully lived up to his fine record of service.

Efforts were made to get the social side of the Battery going and dances were held. A Battery Cup was presented for the best relief on projector drill and this was won by " G " Relief (Capt. R. Henderson) and the cup winning night will long be remembered. A " knock-out " cricket competition was arranged and this was a great success the Sports Cup being won by " F " Relief (Capt. A. Joynes) whose team included several well known players, two of them " County " men. An excellent ·22 rifle team was got together under the command of Capt. R. Hammond. Matches were arranged against all comers, including all G.S. battalions, and the Battery team was victorious in 9 out of 10 matches. After the " clear out " of unsuitable men a very fine spirit prevailed in the Battery, especially among the officers and the unit received high praise from visiting officers. It is specially interesting to record that all the transferees from G.S. units thoroughly enjoyed their experience with the Battery and wished their transfers had been effected earlier. The thanks of the Command are due to the employers of the district, especially to the officers of the G.W.R. Company who were at all times only too willing to co-operate and whose help in combating avoidable absence was invaluable.

The " Close Down " order was received with very mixed feeling, a great number of the old hands being of the opinion that they would have liked to stick it out until the war in the west was over. Farewell dinners were arranged for all reliefs and the excellent spirit of the unit was very evident at these functions.

The following is a list of the officers of the Battery, who deserve the highest praise for their work :

Medical Officer : Maj. D. Dangerfield
" *A* " *Relief* : Capt. G. J. Phipps, Lt. J. T. Knightley, Lt. W. C. Moorcroft, 2/Lt. R. Kerr, C/O. A. Wills, C/O. J. G. Bailey.
" *B* " *Relief* : Capt. W. H. Scribbins, Lt. H. G. Nicolson, Lt. E. V. Carter, 2/Lt. R. L. Barling, 2/Lt. F. O. Jefferson, C/O. F. Allen.
" *C* " *Relief* : Capt. G. H. Staniforth, Lt. D. S. F. Williams, Lt. J. H. Shirley, 2/Lt. S. J. Robinson, C/O. F. H. Booker, C/O. R. D. Colborne
" *D* " *Relief* : Capt. W. Beardmore, Lt. S. A. Leonard, Lt. H. Kaye, 2/Lt. R. R. Colman, 2/Lt. L. E. Taylor, C/O. H. E. Lane.

" *E* " *Relief* : Capt. R. J. Hammond, Lt. E. H. Ferris, Lt. S. W. Cox, 2/Lt. A. A. Sharpe, 2/Lt. V. G. Hepper, C/O. S. C. Casson, C/O. J. F. A. Boalch.
" *F* " *Relief* : Capt. A. Joynes, Lt. H. J. Hubble, Lt. J. G. Rooke, 2/Lt. W. H. Sargent, C/O. H. Easthope.
" *G* " *Relief* : Capt. R. Henderson, Lt. W. C. James, Lt. F. H. Nethercot, 2/Lt. W. G. Howell, C/O. H. J. Ellis.
" *H* " *Relief* : Capt. J. S. Barnes, M.M., Lt. A. J. Towill, Lt. L. J. Hollis, 2/Lt. S. H. B. Honey, 2/Lt. R. C. Mitchell, C/O. E. Hedger, C/O. C. West.

The following awards have been made to members of the unit and further recommendations have been forwarded to the appropriate authority.

British Empire Medal : Pte. Frankis, W. E.

Meritorious Service Certificate : Col.-Sgt. Burden, E ; Col.-Sgt. Casson, S. C. ; Col.-Sgt. Newson, H.

S. J. HARRIS,
Major, Home Guard, Officer Commanding
220th (101st Wiltshire Home Guard) Rocket A.A. Battery

Kingsdown Camp,
Stratton St. Margaret
Near Swindon.
1 *Nov*. 1944

2142 (WILTSHIRE) HOME GUARD M.T. COMPANY

First steps towards the formation of a Home Guard Mechanical Transport Company for the County of Wiltshire were taken in February 1942. Prior to that date, Officer Commanding, Royal Army Service Corps, Salisbury Plain District, had listed certain vehicles in the area which could be usefully mobilised as additional Army transport in an emergency.

Maj. F. R. Way, O.B.E., was entrusted with the formation of the Company, was appointed to command with effect from 27th March 1942 and has continued in command throughout.

Original title was " Wiltshire Home Guard M.T. Company "; then " ' P ' (Wiltshire) Home Guard M.T. Company " and eventually in January—2142 (Wiltshire) Home Guard M.T. Company.

Original establishment, based on Regular R.A.S.C. transport companies was :

Headquarters
3 Transport platoons
1 Workshop platoon
1 Relief drivers platoon

with a vehicle and motor-cycle strength of 161.

Using the vehicles listed by Officer Commanding, Royal Army Service Corps, Salisbury Plain District prior to 1942, as a necleus, all vehicles required to complete the establishment and make the Company operationally effective, were inspected, selected and earmarked within a very short period and in practically every case the normal drivers of such vehicles were enrolled (or transferred where already members of a Home Guard G.S. battalion) as members of the Company. The establishment strength of the Company in personnel was completed by voluntary enrolment. The Workshops Section was enrolled by May 1942 and within a short time of that date, the Company was complete.

In January 1943, the establishment was altered by eliminating the Workshop Platoon and increasing the transport, viz. :

Headquarters
4 Transport platoons
Relief driver increment

increasing the vehicle strength to 199 and reducing the personnel to 273. The necessary further earmarkings of vehicles and adjustment of personnel was completed by March 1943.

Coincident with the alteration in the establishment, 64 affiliated cars for use of Command Headquarters were attached to the Company.

Headquarters of the Company remained at Salisbury throughout and centres for the platoon and R.D.I. headquarters were sited at Salisbury, Swindon, Trowbridge, Warminster and Upavon.

All training was carried out to align with Regular Royal Army Service Corps practice, in conjunction with and under the general supervision of Officer Commanding, Royal Army Service Corps, Salisbury Plain District, Bulford.

On 6th July 1943 the Company was inspected at Wilton by Maj.-Gen. H. R. Kerr, O.B.E., M.C., Director of Supplies and Transport, War Office, who highly praised the Company for its efficient display and smart turnout.

Had " action stations " occurred, the Company would have been attached to and under the immediate direction of Officer Commanding, Royal Army Service Corps, Salisbury Plain District and the operational rôle of the Company was to augment R.A.S.C. services in the Command area.

Company Commanding Officer :
Maj. F. R. Way, O.B.E.
Headquarters : Capt. K. R. C. Holman, Capt. F. C. G. Hill, 2/Lt. C. C. J. Kempster (appointed Sept. 1944 to succeed Lt. W. Moreton, No. 2 Platoon, resigned owing to pressure of work)
Platoon Commanders : Lt. G. W. T. Butt, M.C., Lt. W. Moreton, Lt, K. F. Green, 2/Lt. C. R. T. Swatton. Sgt. T. Atkinson.

In December 1945 came the order for final disbandment, which was to take place on 31st December at midnight.

For the last time the officers and men of Britain's Home Guard met in town and village halls, remembering the last eventful years a little wistfully and determined that the comradeship formed should endure through the years to come.

EPILOGUE
31 Dec. 1945

written by
CAPT. W. LOVELL HEWITT
and played in the Drill Hall
Trowbridge

ANNOUNCER. At midnight the Home Guard will be finally disbanded. In ten minutes time with the old year—the last of the war years—it will fade away. Memories of it will fade, too. But those of us who served in it will never entirely forget. We have asked our Second in Command to give us a five minutes impression of those five long and dramatic years. He has had difficult tasks before, but none more difficult than this. Let's see how he has tackled the job. He has called it— " Do you Remember ? "

(All lights out—spotlight on platform. Roll of drums.)

VOICE. The-month-of-May-nineteen-hundred-and-forty——

RACONTEUR. Denmark annexed. Norway over-run. Holland subjugated. Belgium conquered. The epic of Dunkirk. The fall of France. The Hun 18 miles from Dover—do you remember ? A desperate Britain bares her teeth. Her effective Army 15,000 infantry, 60 tanks AND do you remember ?

(Enter Local Defence Volunteer with F.S. cap, brassard, and hammer shotgun.)

RACONTEUR. One hundred and fifty thousand Local Defence Volunteers were called for. In two weeks there were 400,000. In six weeks a million. With shotguns and cudgels they wait through the star-studded nights. While the voice across the Channel snarles, " Look your last on all things lovely." One cries " Let 'em come,"—another prays " Let me take but one of them with me." and yet the Summer and the Autumn passed—do you remember ?

(Soft roll of drums. Exit Local Defence Volunteer.—Spotlights out for 3 seconds. Roll of drums.)

VOICE. Nineteen-hundred-and-forty-one.

RACONTEUR. Nights of terror. Days of toil. None to share the burden. The Hun is 18 miles from Dover. But troops must go to Africa. And leave the home unguarded ? Unguarded ? Don't you remember ?

(Enter Home Guard in denims, D.S. cap with badge. Rifle.)

One and a half millions of him now. Eight hundred thousand rifles from America—the rest lie on the ocean-bed in the Western Approaches. Grimly, unrelentingly, he toils. Weapon training, patrols, weapon training. His the home to guard. And ever an anxious ear to the news from Russia. If she falls—— The summer and the autumn pass. Russia hangs on. Crete. Pearl Harbour. Do you remember ?

(Soft roll of drums. Exit Home Guard. Spot-lights off for 3 seconds. Roll of drums.)

VOICE. Nineteen-hundred-and-forty-two.

RACONTEUR. Disaster upon disaster. Hong-Kong. Singapore. The Hun in Egypt and still 18 miles from Dover. More troops must go East. There must be more to guard the home—do you remember?

(Enter Home Guard. B.D., S.H., G.M. and Sten.)

A soldier now—two millions of him. And still he toils. Weapon training, exercises, weapon training. On his own ground a match for most of them. Doing his duty with the dignity born of competence. A worker by day. A soldier by night. A salute to you, my friend.

(Soft roll of drums. Exit Home Guard. Spot-lights off for 3 seconds. Roll of drums.)

VOICE. Nineteen-hundred-and-forty-three.

RACONTEUR. On the up-grade now. Rommel out of Africa. Montgomery in Italy. The Yanks are coming. The second front—do you remember? When? Where? How? Every soldier will be wanted. Britain must be left in the care of the Home Guard.

(Enter Home Guard in full marching order—rifle and fixed bayonet.)

Well trained, well equipped. There he waits in tremendous numbers for the task that may never come—just because he *is* there well trained, well equipped in overwhelming strength. Through 1943. Into 1944. Guarding vital communications. Awaiting the counter-stroke to " D " Day—the stroke that was never made largely because of him. And so to the autumn and Stand Down. Rest at last to the civilian-soldier, unique in our history. Truly he has deserved well of his country. His reward—the greatest of rewards—was that he did his duty. And so at midnight to-night to disbandment.

VOICE OFF. Company—dismiss.

(Home Guard comes to attention. Roll of drums and fanfare. Slopes arms. Turns to right. Salutes. Exit.)

RACONTEUR. And here he leaves gladly, but also a little sadly, the great company of those who also served.

(All lights on.)

Ladies and gentlemen. It lacks but a few seconds to midnight. The future lies before us. Remembering the spirit of those great days let's all join hands and welcome in—with Auld Lang Syne—1946.

> No easy hopes or lies
> Shall bring us to our goal,
> But iron sacrifice
> Of body, will, and soul.
> There is but one task for all—
> For each one life to give.
> Who stands if freedom fall?
> Who dies if England live?

Printed and Published by
B. Lansdown & Sons, Ltd.
Duke Street, Trowbridge

14035605R00087

Printed in Great Britain
by Amazon